CROCKERY COOKBOOK

CROCKERY COOKBOOK

Mary Berry

CHARTWELL
BOOKS INC.

Jacket photograph: Hearty Vegetable Soup (page 17)

ISBN 0 89009-143-9
Library of Congress Catalog Card Number 77-80281

Published by Chartwell Books Inc.,
A Division of Book Sales Inc.,
110 Enterprise Avenue,
Secaucus, New Jersey 07094

Contents

Useful Facts and Figures

Notes on metrication

Exact conversion from Imperial to metric measures does not give very convenient working quantities and so for greater ease I have rounded off the metric measures into units of 25. The following tables show recommended equivalents.

Dry measures

Ounces	Approx. g to nearest whole figure	Recommended equivalent to nearest unit of 25
1	28	25
2	57	50
3	85	75
4 ($\frac{1}{4}$ lb)	113	100
5	142	150
6	170	175
7	198	200
8 ($\frac{1}{2}$ lb)	227	225
9	255	250
10	283	275
11	312	300
12 ($\frac{3}{4}$ lb)	340	350
13	368	375
14	397	400
15	425	425
16 (1 lb)	456	450 (or 0.5 kg)

Liquid measures

Fluid ounces	Approx. ml to nearest whole figure	Recommended equivalent to nearest unit of 25
5 ($\frac{1}{4}$ pint)	142	150
6	170	175
7	198	200
8	227	225
9	255	250
10 ($\frac{1}{2}$ pint)	283	300
11	312	325
12	340	350
15 ($\frac{3}{4}$ pint)	425	450
20 (1 pint)	569	600

Below are recommended equivalents for larger, commonly used liquid amounts.

1$\frac{1}{4}$ pints	750 ml
1$\frac{1}{2}$ pints	900 ml
1$\frac{3}{4}$ pints	1 litre
2 pints	generous litre
2$\frac{1}{4}$ pints	1.25 litres
2$\frac{3}{4}$ pints	1.5 litres
3 pints	1.75 litres
3$\frac{1}{2}$ pints	2 litres

Note This method of conversion gives good results in nearly all recipes; however, in certain recipes a more accurate conversion may be necessary to produce a balanced proportion of ingredients.

All spoon measures are level unless otherwise indicated.

Notes for American users

The most important differences between British and American measures are that the Imperial pint is 20 fl oz whereas the American pint is 16 fl oz; the British Standard tablespoon holds 17.7 ml while the American tablespoon holds 14.2 ml. Below are equivalents for a few commonly used amounts.

British	American
1 tablespoon (3 teaspoons)	1 tablespoon (3 teaspoons)
1$\frac{1}{2}$ tablespoons	2 tablespoons
2 tablespoons	3 tablespoons
3 tablespoons	$\frac{1}{4}$ cup
4 tablespoons	$\frac{1}{3}$ cup
5 tablespoons	6 tablespoons
6 tablespoons	$\frac{1}{2}$ cup (4 fl oz)
$\frac{1}{4}$ pint	$\frac{2}{3}$ cup
6 fl oz	$\frac{3}{4}$ cup
scant $\frac{1}{2}$ pint	1 cup (8 fl oz)
$\frac{1}{2}$ pint	1$\frac{1}{4}$ cups
$\frac{3}{4}$ pint	2 cups (1 US pint)
1 pint	2$\frac{1}{2}$ cups

Below is a list of American equivalents for some of the terms and equipment used in this book.

BRITISH/AMERICAN
Baking tin/Baking pan
Base/Bottom
Biscuits (plain or sweet)/Crackers or cookies
Cocktail stick/Toothpick
Deep cake tin/Spring form pan
Dough or mixture/Batter
Frying pan/Skillet
Greaseproof paper/Wax paper
Grill/Broiler
Kitchen paper/Paper towels
Liquidiser/Blender
Loaf tin/Loaf pan
Minced/Ground
Muslin/Cheesecloth
Pastry cutter/Cookie cutter
Piping bag/Pastry bag
Polythene/Plastic
Pudding basin/Ovenproof bowl
Salt beef/Corned beef
Sandwich tin/Layer cake pan
Scones/Biscuits
Stoned/Pitted
Swiss roll/Jelly roll
Top and tail fruit/Stem fruit
Whip (eggs and cream)/Beat
Whisk/Whip
Wholemeal/Wholewheat

Notes for Australian users
In Australia the American 8-oz measuring cup is used in conjunction with the Imperial pint of 20 fl oz. It is most important to remember that the Australian tablespoon differs from both the British and American tablespoons in that it holds 20 ml. The table below gives a comparison.

British	Australian
1 teaspoon	1 teaspoon
1 tablespoon	1 tablespoon
2 tablespoons	2 tablespoons
$3\frac{1}{2}$ tablespoons	3 tablespoons
4 tablespoons	$3\frac{1}{2}$ tablespoons

Recipe conversion
The table below gives a guide to converting recipe cooking times from conventional cookers to electric slow cookers.

Conventional cooking time	Slow cooking time	
	LOW	HIGH
15–30 minutes	4–8 hours	$1\frac{1}{2}$–$2\frac{1}{2}$ hours
30 minutes – 1 hour	6–8 hours	3–4 hours
1–3 hours	8–16 hours	4–6 hours

Note As a general rule, allow twice the slow cooking time when converting from the HIGH to the LOW setting.

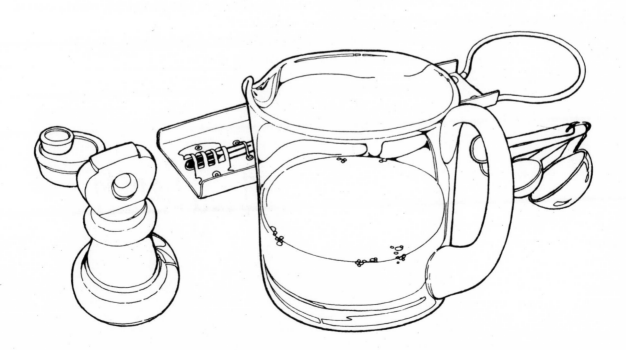

Introduction

Why, in this modern age of speed, is there so much interest in slow cooking? I think the main reason is that slow cooked food tastes good — strongly followed by the important advantages of convenience and economy. Long, gentle cooking results in tender, succulent dishes, full of the natural flavours of the food and seasonings. These delicious results would make any slow cooking appliance intriguing.

Then there is the convenience of preparing a meal whenever you like, beginning the cooking process then going out to work or shop for the day — and finally coming home to a delicious meal, perfectly cooked and piping hot!

The clinching argument for most of us these days is, of course, economy. Slow cooking brings out the truly appetising qualities of cheaper cuts of meat, adds interest to standard ways of cooking vegetables like potatoes, and easily produces family favourites like porridge and rice pudding.

One of the most convenient, economical and safest methods of cooking food slowly is in an electric slow cooker. Designed to perform the job efficiently using a minimum of electricity, this modern appliance is a real boon to cooks, whether working wives, busy mothers or imaginative hostesses. I used all the slow cookers currently on the market in this country in the course of testing the recipes in this book, and I can recommend the appliance without reservation.

Slow cooking can be imaginative and creative as well as convenient. This aspect will become more apparent as you gain experience in the methods involved, and may in time become the biggest advantage of all.

But do try all the recipes in this book, and do adapt and invent your own. The advantages of one pot cooking are a matter of personal opinion — you won't know which benefit you most until you get to know your own slow cooker. It can be a worthwhile friend in the kitchen!

I would like to take this opportunity to thank Clare Blunt, whose meticulous recipe development work is gratefully appreciated.

Mary Berry.

ALL ABOUT ONE POT COOKING

Let's face it: very few women really want to spend all day in the kitchen cooking meals. Most of us would rather be with the family, or at work earning extra money, or pursuing any of the dozens of activities we would like to try if only we had the time.

Convenience foods, pressure cookers and high-speed grills have all offered means of releasing the housewife from the shackles of the kitchen stove. Now we have a fourth — one pot cookery — which tackles the problem from a totally different angle. The others use rapid speed as the fundamental principle. With one pot cookery, the idea is slow and easy, so that the pot can get on with the job of cooking the food while the cook is elsewhere enjoying herself.

Principles

Most slow cookers on the market work along the same lines. They consist of a stoneware or earthenware casserole which is contained within an outer casing fitted with a heating element. When the cooker, which is powered by electricity, is turned on — most have two settings, high and low — the *contents* of the casserole are slowly heated to simmering point and kept at this temperature (never hotter than 100°C/212°F) for as long as the cooker remains on. Most low settings maintain a continuous *appliance* temperature ranging from 82°C/180°F to 93°C/200°F, while the high setting maintains a temperature of 150°C/300°F.

Gentle heat acting on the food for several hours tenderises it and extracts the maximum flavour. Gristly meat softens and fruit and vegetables retain their shape. Slow cookers are fantastic for cooking tricky fruits like rhubarb or gooseberries so that their colour is good and the texture perfect. Because the amount of energy required to keep the casserole at a low, even temperature is small, very little electricity is used and the cookers are very economical to run.

The principle of slow cookery is, of course, nothing new. Our ancestors used a haybox, which was a somewhat haphazard method but usually effective. It was also inherently unsafe because of the constantly falling temperature and subsequent danger from bacteria. The modern slow cooker leaves nothing to chance as the temperature is kept at a safe level, so there is no danger of contamination of food. Extensive research has been carried out by the manufacturers to ensure that the cooking process is sufficient to destroy all harmful bacteria. Furthermore, it is an attractive piece of kitchen equipment, which you can take to the table for serving, and takes up little space on a worktop, where it is always ready to use when you want it.

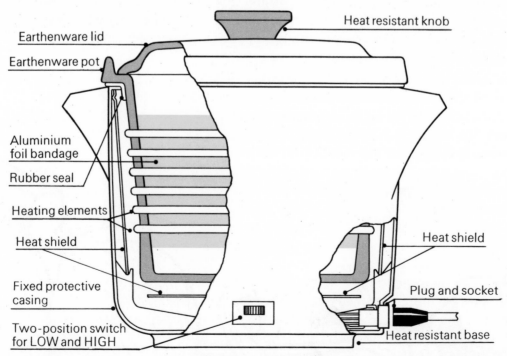

Heat resistant knob

Earthenware lid

Earthenware pot

Aluminium foil bandage

Rubber seal

Heating elements

Heat shield

Heat shield

Fixed protective casing

Plug and socket

Two-position switch for LOW and HIGH

Heat resistant base

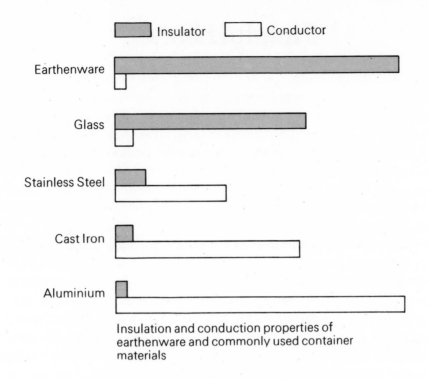

Insulation and conduction properties of earthenware and commonly used container materials

Rules to Remember

Before trying a slow cooker for the first time, there are a few rules to remember. The first is to *read the manufacturer's instructions carefully*. Not all the inner containers are oven- or dishwasher-proof and they cannot, therefore, double as additional casserole dishes. Only one can be put under the grill to brown the top of the food. Some can be used to cook food (but *never* poultry) from frozen. The capacity of the pot is important, too: some hold approximately 2 litres/3½ pints (US 4½ pints), which should be sufficient for 4–6 servings, while others hold twice that amount. Whatever the size, the pot should be at least half full for best results (if not, remember to check the timing).

Pay particular attention to the length of cooking time given in each recipe. Since you cannot overcook the food, it doesn't matter one bit if the dish cooks on high for up to 2 hours longer than mentioned in the recipe or on low for up to 4 hours longer. However, it *is* perfectly possible to undercook. If you cut the meat up in larger pieces than suggested in the recipe, cook it for longer to be sure of the best results. Also, be sure to trim any excess fat from the meat before slow cooking, as too much fat could increase the temperature and will not 'cook away'. The recipe times have been studiously worked out as a guide to best results. These have been noted separately for convenience in choosing a dish to fit in with your schedule.

Do not be tempted to peep at the dish whilst it is cooking. Removing the lid reduces the temperature and means that longer cooking time, usually an additional 15–20 minutes, would be required. In any case, peeping will not give you much information. The cooking temperature is so low that there is little movement of the liquid. Stirring is unnecessary except in a very few cases, i.e. cooking rice or fondue, when this is noted in the recipe.

Helpful Hints

Stick to the quantity of liquid given in the recipe, even though it is less than you would normally use for a particular dish. There is no loss of liquid during cooking with a slow cooker because there is no evaporation. If you are adapting your own recipes, cut the normal quantity of liquid by about half. Rice and pasta dishes need from a quarter to a third less liquid (pasta requires short pre-cooking, just to soften it, before adding it to the pot).

Reduce seasoning slightly and use a smaller amount of herbs and spices than you usually do. Slow cooking enhances flavours and you do not want your dish to taste as though you had emptied the whole spice jar in by mistake. Whole herbs and spices take longer to release their flavour than ground (which dissipate over a long period), thus giving a stronger taste. Dairy ingredients like fresh or soured cream should always be added at the end, as prolonged cooking causes them to separate and curdle.

Most dishes require a certain amount of pre-cooking but no more than is necessary with conventional methods. Braising meat, stewing steak, etc. are best if browned in the frying pan first. It also helps to heat stock or sauce to boiling in a separate pan before pouring it into the pot, although some makes cook very efficiently from cold. Others work best when preheated. *Read your own instruction book and check first any special points regarding your slow cooker.*

Planning Meals

Users of slow cookers will probably have to re-plan their household routine, always remembering that it is the *minimum* cooking time which is important. To have their evening meal waiting in the pot ready to serve when they get in from work is a great boon to working wives. But if your weakness is getting up in the morning so that you habitually leave the house in a rush and wash up the breakfast things when you get home, you will have to prepare the dish the evening before. The food should then be refrigerated in a separate container overnight, never left out in the pot. Midday meals need the same advance preparation. Porridge for breakfast can be started the night before and left to cook safely whilst you sleep. This is particularly useful for mothers of schoolchildren; if they can help themselves whilst you organise caps/satchels/bus money, etc., a great deal of nervous energy is saved. Rolls for breakfast can also be heated in the slow cooker.

There are, in fact, many advantages to one pot cooking once you have trained yourself to the new routine. Casseroles and similar dishes will stay hot for up to 2 hours on low so that latecomers to meals can still get a fresh, perfectly done serving. Because of the long, slow cooking involved, there is less shrinkage of the meat so that what you buy will go further. Vegetables will cook with the meat without breaking up, thus giving the food a more appetising appearance. Cooking canned frankfurters is particularly successful as they will heat through without bursting.

Safety

Finally, a word about safety. All the slow cookers on the market are electrically operated and should therefore be treated with the care you would normally use when dealing with electrical appliances in the kitchen. Never, for example, immerse the electrical parts in water. They should conform to recognised criteria such as British Standards. If your cooker has a removable pot, it may get quite hot when the cooker is switched on, and using oven gloves when handling the pot is advisable.

From a health point of view, there are no hazards. You should still, however, use your common sense. Do not, for example, attempt to cook a frozen chicken in the pot without making certain that it has thawed out completely in the refrigerator first. Chicken in any case should never be cooked from the frozen state.

The joy of the slow cooker lies in the time it saves you to spend elsewhere. As you will see from the recipes that follow, there are a surprising number and variety of dishes which can be cooked in it: no doubt you will soon be adding your own ideas to the list. A chart for converting your favourite recipes from conventional to slow electric cookers appears on page 7. Once a few simple guidelines are mastered, the versatility, economy and convenience of slow cooking will make it an essential aid to all your meal planning.

opposite *Cornish Crab Soup*
(page 16)

SOUPS

Stock forms the basis of most recipes which call for liquid in the cooking. Yet many housewives prefer to rely on the stock cube rather than make the stock themselves. I suspect that the reason lies in the bother of stockmaking, the feeling that whilst it is cooking gently on the stove the kitchen cannot be left unattended in case the pan boils dry or the cat knocks it over. This, of course, is where the slow cooker scores. It cannot boil dry and it would need a small tiger to upset it. You can leave the house in complete safety while the stock is cooking and return several hours later to find the job done. I find that the best way to make stock is to let it cook overnight; then it is ready to use for a recipe the next day or to freeze in the freezer. However, stock cubes can of course be substituted if you have not recently cooked a whole bird or joint.

The following recipes describe the method for making stocks and give suggestions for soups which are dependent on a good, tasty stock. Many of the soups are ideal for using up garden vegetables and all are sure to be popular with the whole family, whether served as a starter to a main meal or as part of a light but filling lunch or supper in summer and winter alike.

Chicken Stock

METRIC/IMPERIAL
chicken carcass
chicken giblets and skin
1 onion, sliced
parsley stalk
bay leaf
½ teaspoon salt
boiling water

A very good way to make stock – all the smells stay in the pot and the long slow cooking makes a stock full of flavour.

Place the carcass, giblets and skin in the slow cooker with the onion, parsley, bay leaf and seasoning, and pour over just sufficient boiling water to cover the bones. Cover the pot and cook on LOW for 7–8 hours. Strain the stock into a bowl and leave to cool. Lift off any fat when cold, then use as required.

Slow cooking time: 7–8 hours

AMERICAN
chicken carcass
chicken giblets and skin
1 onion, sliced
parsley stalk
bay leaf
½ teaspoon salt
boiling water

Turkey and Onion Soup

METRIC/IMPERIAL
Stock:
turkey carcass
1 onion, sliced
bay leaf
parsley stalk
1 teaspoon salt
900 ml/1½ pints boiling water

40 g/1½ oz butter
225 g/8 oz onions, chopped
40 g/1½ oz cornflour
300 ml/½ pint milk
2 teaspoons chopped fresh
 tarragon or chives
salt and pepper

No need to wait until Christmas to make this soup: if you haven't got a turkey, use two chicken carcasses instead.

Break the carcass so that it will fit in the slow cooker, add the remaining stock ingredients, cover and cook on LOW for 7–8 hours. Strain and measure the stock to make up 1 litre/1¾ pints (US 2 pints). Pick meat from the carcass.
 Melt the butter in a large saucepan, add the onion, cover and cook gently until soft but not brown; this will take about 20 minutes. Blend the cornflour with the milk and stir into the pan with the stock, bring to the boil, stirring, and simmer for 3–4 minutes. Add the turkey meat, fresh herbs and seasoning to taste.

Serves 8
Slow cooking time: 7–8 hours

AMERICAN
Stock:
turkey carcass
1 onion, sliced
bay leaf
parsley stalk
1 teaspoon salt
3¾ cups boiling water

3 tablespoons butter
½ lb onions, chopped
⅓ cup cornstarch
1¼ cups milk
2 teaspoons chopped fresh
 tarragon or chives
salt and pepper

Cornish Crab Soup

METRIC/IMPERIAL
25 g/1 oz butter
225 g/8 oz vegetables, finely
 chopped, to include:
 carrots, onions and celery
2 teaspoons tomato purée
salt and pepper
600 ml/1 pint water
100-g/3½-oz can crabmeat
4 tablespoons top milk
1 tablespoon chopped parsley

A delicious soup, full of flavour – make and serve it for a special dinner party.

Melt the butter in a frying pan, add the vegetables and cook for about 5 minutes without browning. Add the tomato purée, seasoning and water and bring to the boil. Turn into the slow cooker, cover and cook on HIGH for 1½ hours or until the vegetables are soft.
 Drain and flake the crabmeat, removing any small pieces of bone, and add with the milk to the pot. Stir in the parsley. Taste to check the seasoning, cover the pot and heat on HIGH for a further 30 minutes. Serve with chunks of French bread.

Serves 2–3
Slow cooking time: 2 hours

AMERICAN
2 tablespoons butter
½ lb vegetables, finely chopped,
 to include: carrots, onions
 and celery
2 teaspoons tomato paste
salt and pepper
2½ cups water
3½-oz can crabmeat
⅓ cup rich milk
1 tablespoon chopped parsley

Hearty Vegetable Soup

Prepare this soup for the family on a cold winter's day — it makes a meal in itself, served with slices of French bread.

Place the beef in a large saucepan with the water and salt and bring to the boil; skim. Turn into the slow cooker with all the other ingredients except the macaroni and cabbage, roughly chopping the tomatoes. Cover and cook on HIGH for 1 hour, then turn to LOW and cook for a further 6 hours.

Drain the macaroni and add to soup with the cabbage, cover and cook for a further 30 minutes. Lift out the beef and carefully remove the meat from the bone. Shred the meat into small pieces and stir into the soup. Taste to check the seasoning. Sprinkle with chopped parsley before serving.

Serves 6–8
Slow cooking time: 7½ hours

METRIC/IMPERIAL
0.5 kg/1 lb shin of beef with bone
1.75 litres/3 pints water
2 teaspoons salt
1 onion, chopped
100 g/4 oz courgettes, thinly sliced
225 g/8 oz carrots, diced
396-g/14-oz can tomatoes
100 g/4 oz short-cut macaroni, lightly cooked
225 g/8 oz cabbage, finely shredded
chopped parsley to garnish

AMERICAN
1 lb beef foreshank with bone
4 pints water
2 teaspoons salt
1 onion, chopped
¼ lb zucchini, thinly sliced
½ lb carrots, diced
14-oz can tomatoes
1 cup macaroni, lightly cooked
3 cups finely shredded cabbage
chopped parsley to garnish

Scotch Broth

Trim the fat from the lamb and cut meat into pieces. Place in a saucepan with the water and bring to the boil, skim thoroughly and add the pearl barley and salt. Simmer for 20 minutes.

Add the vegetables to the pan with the pepper, bring to the boil again and pour into the slow cooker. Cover and cook on LOW for 3–4 hours. Lift out the meat and remove all bones and marrow. Return the meat to the pot, taste to check the seasoning and serve sprinkled with plenty of chopped parsley.

Serves 6
Slow cooking time: 3–4 hours

METRIC/IMPERIAL
0.5 kg/1 lb neck of lamb
scant 1.5 litres/2½ pints water
50 g/2 oz pearl barley
1 teaspoon salt
2 onions, chopped
2 carrots, diced
2 sticks celery, sliced
½ teaspoon white pepper
chopped parsley to garnish

AMERICAN
1 lb lamb neck slices
6¼ cups water
generous ¼ cup pearl barley
1 teaspoon salt
2 onions, chopped
2 carrots, diced
2 stalks celery, sliced
½ teaspoon white pepper
chopped parsley to garnish

Bouillabaisse

Wash, dry and skin the fish, and cut it into 3.5-cm/1½-inch pieces, removing any bones. Place in the slow cooker with the bay leaf, onion and water. Season well, cover and cook on LOW for 2 hours. Add the tomatoes and prawns and cook for a further 1 hour.

Put the slices of French bread in a soup tureen, check the seasoning and pour the soup over the bread. Sprinkle with plenty of chopped parsley and serve. Or if you prefer, just serve with French or garlic bread.

Serves 6
Slow cooking time: 3 hours

METRIC/IMPERIAL
0.5 kg/1¼ lb mixed white fish, to include: plaice, whiting, bream and mackerel
bay leaf
2 onions, finely chopped
450 ml/¾ pint boiling water
salt and pepper
225 g/8 oz tomatoes, peeled, seeded and chopped
100 g/4 oz peeled prawns
6 slices French bread
chopped parsley to garnish

AMERICAN
1¼ lb mixed white fish, to include: flounder, whiting and mackerel
bay leaf
2 onions, finely chopped
2 cups boiling water
salt and pepper
½ lb tomatoes, peeled, seeded and chopped
⅔ cup shelled shrimp
6 slices French bread
chopped parsley to garnish

Celery Soup

METRIC/IMPERIAL
25 g/1 oz butter
1 onion, chopped
1 head celery
225 g/8 oz potatoes, sliced
900 ml/1½ pints chicken stock
1 teaspoon salt
freshly ground black pepper
150 ml/¼ pint single cream or
   top milk

Melt the butter in a saucepan, add the onion and fry gently for 5 minutes. Wash and finely slice the celery and add to the pan with the potatoes; add the stock and seasoning and bring to the boil. Turn into the slow cooker, cover and cook on HIGH for 30 minutes, then turn to LOW for 8 hours or until the celery is really tender.

Turn the soup into a liquidiser or rub through a sieve until it becomes a smooth purée. Rinse out the pot and return the soup to it; turn to HIGH. Taste to check the seasoning and, when hot and ready to serve, stir in the cream.

AMERICAN
2 tablespoons butter
1 onion, chopped
1 bunch celery
½ lb potatoes, sliced
3¾ cups chicken stock
1 teaspoon salt
freshly ground black pepper
⅔ cup light cream or rich milk

Serves 4–6
Slow cooking time: 9 hours

Rich Vegetable Soup

METRIC/IMPERIAL
225 g/8 oz leeks, well washed
50 g/2 oz butter
2 onions, finely sliced
4 sticks celery, finely sliced
2 large potatoes, finely sliced
25 g/1 oz plain flour
600 ml/1 pint chicken stock
300 ml/½ pint milk
salt and pepper
pinch grated nutmeg

If you have a large slow cooker, double this recipe, eat one batch and freeze the rest for another meal.

Finely slice both the white and the green parts of the leeks. Melt the butter in a pan, add the leeks with the other vegetables and cook gently, covered, for about 10 minutes without browning. Stir in the flour and cook for 2 minutes, add the stock and bring to the boil, stirring. Add the milk and seasoning, reheat and turn into the slow cooker; cover and cook on HIGH for 30 minutes, then turn to LOW and cook for a further 4 hours.

Purée the soup in a liquidiser. Rinse out the pot and reheat the soup in it on HIGH. Taste to check the seasoning and serve.

AMERICAN
½ lb leeks, well washed
¼ cup butter
2 onions, finely sliced
4 stalks celery, finely sliced
2 large potatoes, finely sliced
¼ cup all-purpose flour
2½ cups chicken stock
1¼ cups milk
salt and pepper
pinch grated nutmeg

Serves 4
Slow cooking time: 5 hours

opposite *Celery Soup and Rich Vegetable Soup*

Dutch Pea Soup

METRIC/IMPERIAL
225 g/8 oz split green peas
generous litre/2 pints water
1 gammon knuckle
1 onion, sliced
bay leaf
1 tablespoon chopped parsley
salt and pepper
knob of butter

Put the peas in a bowl with enough water to cover and leave to soak for 5–6 hours. Drain and put in the slow cooker with the measured water, gammon knuckle, onion and bay leaf. Cover and cook on LOW for 12–14 hours (overnight is ideal for this soup as the peas need a long slow cooking time).

Lift out the gammon knuckle, discard the skin and cut the meat into neat pieces. Discard the bay leaf, place the soup in a liquidiser and reduce it to a purée. Return to the pot with the meat, parsley and seasoning and heat through on HIGH for 30 minutes. Taste to check the seasoning and add the knob of butter. Serve piping hot with crusty rolls or French bread.

AMERICAN
1 cup split green peas
2½ pints water
1 pig's knuckle
1 onion, sliced
bay leaf
1 tablespoon chopped parsley
salt and pepper
knob of butter

Serves 6
Slow cooking time: 12½–14½ hours

Artichoke Soup

METRIC/IMPERIAL
0.75 kg/1½ lb Jerusalem
   artichokes
25 g/1 oz butter
100 g/4 oz onions, chopped
900 ml/1½ pints chicken stock
1 teaspoon salt
½ teaspoon dried sage
freshly ground black pepper
chopped parsley or fried bacon
   snippets to garnish

A lovely, warming winter soup, full of flavour.

Wash the artichokes, put them in a saucepan, cover with cold water and bring to the boil. Simmer for 10 minutes, drain well and peel.

Rinse out the saucepan, melt the butter in it and add onion. Cook for 5 minutes, add the artichokes and remaining ingredients and bring to the boil. Turn into the slow cooker, cover and cook on HIGH for 30 minutes, then turn to LOW and cook for 5–6 hours or until tender. (The time will vary a little depending on the size and age of the artichokes.) Allow the soup to cool slightly.

Purée the soup in a liquidiser, then rinse out the slow cooker and return the soup to it. Heat through on HIGH until piping hot, taste to check the seasoning and serve, sprinkled with chopped parsley or snippets of fried bacon.

AMERICAN
1½ lb Jerusalem artichokes
2 tablespoons butter
¼ lb onions, chopped
3¾ cups chicken stock
1 teaspoon salt
½ teaspoon dried sage
freshly ground black pepper
chopped parsley or fried bacon
   snippets to garnish

Serves 4–6
Slow cooking time: 6–7 hours

Cauliflower Soup

METRIC/IMPERIAL
25 g/1 oz butter
1 onion, chopped
1 small cauliflower
450 ml/¾ pint chicken stock
salt and pepper
25 g/1 oz cornflour
300 ml/½ pint milk
chopped parsley or chives to
  garnish

Melt the butter in a saucepan and fry the onion until soft.

Wash the cauliflower, cut in four and remove the thick stem and leaves. Break the cauliflower into small florets, add to the pan and cook for 2 minutes, add the stock and bring to the boil; season well. Turn into the slow cooker, cover and cook on HIGH for 30 minutes. Turn to LOW and cook for a further 5 hours.

Carefully strain the cauliflower and put on one side. Measure the chicken stock and if necessary make up to 600 ml/1 pint (US 2½ cups) with water. Blend the cornflour with the milk and place in a pan, add the stock and bring to the boil, stirring, and simmer for a few minutes or until thickened. Taste to check seasoning and stir in the cauliflower. Sprinkle with a little chopped parsley or chives before serving.

Serves 4
Slow cooking time: 5½ hours

AMERICAN
2 tablespoons butter
1 onion, chopped
1 small cauliflower
2 cups chicken stock
salt and pepper
¼ cup cornstarch
1¼ cups milk
chopped parsley or chives to
  garnish

Tomato Soup

METRIC/IMPERIAL
40 g/1½ oz butter
1 onion, chopped
50 g/2 oz plain flour
900 ml/1½ pints chicken stock
1 teaspoon salt
freshly ground black pepper
1 teaspoon sugar
0.75 kg/1½ lb tomatoes,
  quartered
1 tablespoon tomato purée
natural yogurt or soured cream
snipped chives to garnish

This is an excellent way to use up soft tomatoes or extra ones from the garden. The long slow cooking brings out their full flavour.

Melt the butter in a pan and fry the onion for 2–3 minutes. Stir in the flour and cook for a further minute. Add the stock; bring to the boil, stirring, and add the seasoning, sugar, tomatoes and tomato purée. Return to the boil and pour into the slow cooker. Cover and cook on LOW for 5–6 hours.

Sieve or liquidise the soup and return it to the pot on HIGH. Heat through for 20–30 minutes. Taste to check the seasoning. Serve with a spoonful of yogurt or soured cream stirred into each bowl and sprinkle with chives.

Serves 6
Slow cooking time: 5½–6½ hours

AMERICAN
3 tablespoons butter
1 onion, chopped
½ cup all-purpose flour
4 cups chicken stock
1 teaspoon salt
freshly ground black pepper
1 teaspoon sugar
1½ lb tomatoes, quartered
1 tablespoon tomato paste
plain yogurt or dairy sour cream
snipped chives to garnish

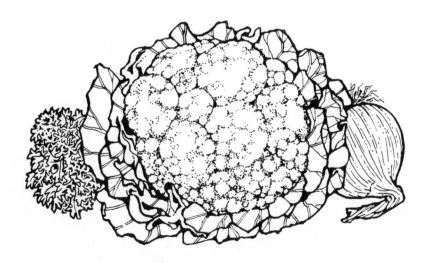

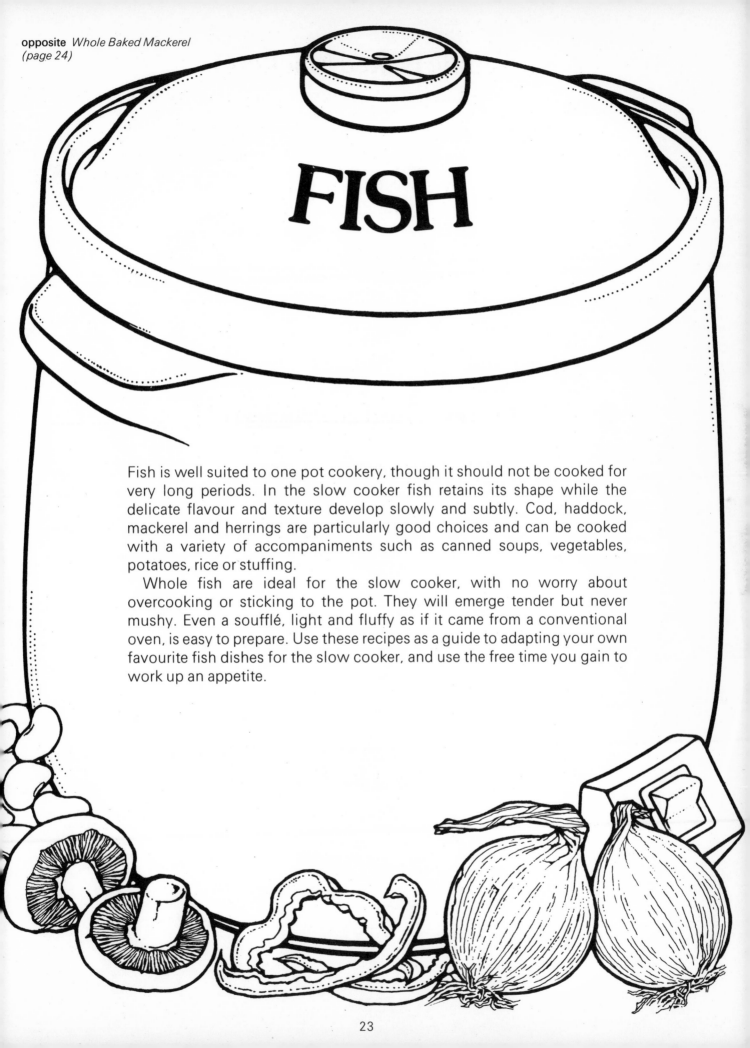

opposite *Whole Baked Mackerel*
(page 24)

FISH

Fish is well suited to one pot cookery, though it should not be cooked for very long periods. In the slow cooker fish retains its shape while the delicate flavour and texture develop slowly and subtly. Cod, haddock, mackerel and herrings are particularly good choices and can be cooked with a variety of accompaniments such as canned soups, vegetables, potatoes, rice or stuffing.

Whole fish are ideal for the slow cooker, with no worry about overcooking or sticking to the pot. They will emerge tender but never mushy. Even a soufflé, light and fluffy as if it came from a conventional oven, is easy to prepare. Use these recipes as a guide to adapting your own favourite fish dishes for the slow cooker, and use the free time you gain to work up an appetite.

Whole Baked Mackerel

A delicious way of serving whole fish. If mackerel are unobtainable, try using trout, herrings or small whole whiting.

Remove the heads from the fish, clean and wash the flesh well. Butter the slow cooker and lay the fish in it; season well and sprinkle with the chopped onion, herbs and lemon juice. Cover and cook on LOW for 2 hours.

If liked, a few whole button mushrooms may be added to the pot for the last 30 minutes of the cooking time.

Serves 4
Slow cooking time: 2 hours

METRIC/IMPERIAL
4 mackerel
50 g/2 oz butter
salt and pepper
1 small onion, finely chopped
1 tablespoon chopped fresh
    mixed herbs
1 tablespoon lemon juice
button mushrooms (optional)

AMERICAN
4 mackerel
¼ cup butter
salt and pepper
1 small onion, finely chopped
1 tablespoon chopped fresh
    mixed herbs
1 tablespoon lemon juice
button mushrooms (optional)

Lemon Stuffed Mackerel

Cut off the head and cut along the underside of each fish to the tail; remove the gut, open the fish and place flesh side down on a board. Press firmly along the backbone, turn over to lift away the bone and cut off the tail.

Place the breadcrumbs in a bowl with the parsley, onion, lemon rind and seasoning and mix well with the egg. Lay the mackerel flat, flesh side up, and place a portion of stuffing on each fish; roll up.

Well butter the slow cooker with half the butter and lay the fish in it. Dot with the remaining butter, cover and cook on LOW for 3½–4 hours.

Serves 4
Slow cooking time: 3½–4 hours

METRIC/IMPERIAL
4 small mackerel
50 g/2 oz butter
Stuffing:
50 g/2 oz fresh white
    breadcrumbs
1 tablespoon chopped parsley
1 tablespoon grated onion
grated rind of 1 lemon
salt and pepper
1 egg, beaten

AMERICAN
4 small mackerel
¼ cup butter
Stuffing:
1 cup fresh white bread crumbs
1 tablespoon chopped parsley
1 tablespoon grated onion
grated rind of 1 lemon
salt and pepper
1 egg, beaten

Fish Hot Pot

Cut the fish into convenient size serving portions and lay them in the slow cooker. Put the soup into a small saucepan with the sherry and pimiento strips and bring to the boil, stirring until evenly blended. Pour over the fish, cover and cook on LOW for 3–4 hours. Taste to check if seasoning is necessary and serve sprinkled with chopped parsley.

Serves 4
Slow cooking time: 3–4 hours

METRIC/IMPERIAL
0.5 kg/1 lb cod or haddock
    fillet
297-g/10½-oz can condensed
    mushroom soup
2 tablespoons sherry
1 canned pimiento, cut
    in strips
salt and pepper (optional)
chopped parsley to garnish

AMERICAN
1 lb cod or haddock filet
10½-oz can condensed
    mushroom soup
3 tablespoons sherry
1 canned pimiento, cut in
    strips
salt and pepper (optional)
chopped parsley to garnish

Cod Steaks Provençale

METRIC/IMPERIAL
4 cod steaks
1 onion, finely chopped
227-g/8-oz can tomatoes
salt and pepper
1 teaspoon oregano
6 stuffed green olives, sliced

Lay the cod steaks in the slow cooker. Place all the other ingredients in a small saucepan and bring to the boil; pour over the fish. Cover and cook on LOW for 3½–4 hours. Taste to check the seasoning and serve with mashed potatoes or rice and a green vegetable.

Serves 4
Slow cooking time: 3½–4 hours

AMERICAN
4 cod steaks
1 onion, finely chopped
8-oz can tomatoes
salt and pepper
1 teaspoon oregano
6 stuffed green olives, sliced

Italian Cod

METRIC/IMPERIAL
1 tablespoon cooking oil
225 g/8 oz courgettes, sliced
1 onion, chopped
1 clove garlic, crushed
225 g/8 oz tomatoes, peeled
  and quartered
salt and pepper
4 cod steaks
0.5 kg/1 lb potatoes, boiled,
  peeled and sliced
butter
chopped parsley to garnish

This is a lovely way of serving cod steaks and is a complete meal in itself.

Heat the oil in a pan, add the courgettes and onion and fry gently for 5–6 minutes. Add the garlic and tomatoes, season well and bring to the boil. Lay the cod steaks in the slow cooker and pour over the hot vegetables. Arrange a layer of sliced potatoes on top and dot with butter, cover and cook on LOW for 4 hours. Serve sprinkled with chopped parsley.

Serves 4
Slow cooking time: 4 hours

AMERICAN
1 tablespoon cooking oil
½ lb zucchini, sliced
1 onion, chopped
1 clove garlic, crushed
½ lb tomatoes, peeled and
  quartered
salt and pepper
4 cod steaks
1 lb potatoes, boiled, peeled
  and sliced
butter
chopped parsley to garnish

Soused Herrings

METRIC/IMPERIAL
6 herrings
salt and pepper
1 small onion, thinly sliced
1 teaspoon peppercorns
bay leaf
6 cloves
150 ml/¼ pint malt vinegar
150 ml/¼ pint water

Clean the herrings and remove the heads and tails. Season the flesh well with salt and pepper and roll up each one. Place in the slow cooker with the remaining ingredients, cover and cook on LOW for 4–5 hours.

Carefully lift out the fish and place in a serving dish. Pour over the cooking liquor and allow to cool, then chill well before serving.

Serves 6
Slow cooking time: 4–5 hours

AMERICAN
6 herring
salt and pepper
1 small onion, thinly sliced
1 teaspoon peppercorns
bay leaf
6 cloves
⅔ cup malt vinegar
⅔ cup water

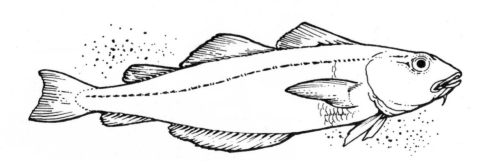

Soused Herrings (page 25)

Baked Haddock Soufflé

METRIC/IMPERIAL
225 g/8 oz smoked haddock
300 ml/½ pint milk
50 g/2 oz butter
50 g/2 oz plain flour
3 large eggs, separated
salt and pepper
boiling water
chopped parsley to garnish

AMERICAN
½ lb smoked haddock
1¼ cups milk
¼ cup butter
½ cup all-purpose flour
3 large eggs, separated
salt and pepper
boiling water
chopped parsley to garnish

This soufflé may be cooked in individual dishes, and will fill 4–6 depending on the size of your slow cooker. Cook on HIGH for 1½–2 hours and serve for lunch with green peas and tomatoes.

Place the haddock in a shallow pan with the milk and simmer for 10 minutes. Strain the milk into a jug, flake the fish and remove any skin or bones.

Well butter a generous litre/2-pint (US 2½-pint) soufflé dish with a little of the butter. Melt the remaining butter in a saucepan and stir in the flour, cook for 2 minutes, add the milk and bring to the boil, stirring. Cook until the roux has thickened. Remove the pan from the heat and beat in the egg yolks one at a time; add the flaked fish and season to taste.

Whisk the egg whites until stiff then fold into the fish mixture. Cover with a piece of buttered foil, slightly domed with a pleat in the centre. Stand the dish in the slow cooker, pour in sufficient boiling water to come halfway up the sides, cover and cook on HIGH for 3–3½ hours. Remove the foil, sprinkle with parsley and serve.

Serves 4
Slow cooking time: 3–3½ hours

Swedish Fish

METRIC/IMPERIAL
1 large mackerel, filleted
350 g/12 oz cod fillet
100 g/4 oz button
  mushrooms, sliced
1 onion, finely chopped
2 tablespoons lemon juice
50 g/2 oz long-grain rice
½ teaspoon salt
freshly ground black pepper
227-g/8-oz can tomatoes
chopped parsley to garnish

AMERICAN
1 large mackerel, fileted
¾ lb cod filet
1 cup button mushrooms,
  sliced
1 onion, finely chopped
3 tablespoons lemon juice
¼ cup long-grain rice
½ teaspoon salt
freshly ground black pepper
8-oz can tomatoes
chopped parsley to garnish

Serve with a green salad or French beans.

Cut the fish into 5-cm/2-inch pieces and lay them in the slow cooker. Put the remaining ingredients except the parsley in a saucepan and bring to the boil, stirring. Pour over the fish, cover and cook on LOW for 3½–4 hours. Check the seasoning and sprinkle with parsley just before serving.

Serves 4
Slow cooking time: 3½–4 hours

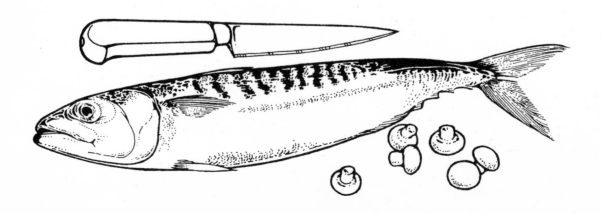

Kedgeree

The slow cooker is excellent for reheating the kedgeree for a crowd when required.

METRIC/IMPERIAL
200 g/7 oz long-grain rice
0.5 kg/1 lb smoked haddock
  fillet
100 g/4 oz butter
3 hard-boiled eggs, chopped
salt and pepper
cayenne pepper

AMERICAN
scant cup long-grain rice
1 lb smoked haddock filet
½ cup butter
3 hard-cooked eggs, chopped
salt and pepper
cayenne pepper

Cook the rice in plenty of boiling salted water; drain and rinse thoroughly.

Line a grill pan with foil, lay the haddock on it, dot with half the butter and grill under a medium grill for 8–10 minutes. Reserve the fish juices, remove any skin and bones from the haddock and flake the fish.

Thoroughly butter the slow cooker with the remaining butter and add the rice, haddock and chopped eggs with seasoning to taste. Stir lightly to mix. Cover, turn the slow cooker to LOW and heat for 2½–4 hours. Taste to check the seasoning, and sprinkle with a little extra cayenne before serving.

Serves 6
Slow cooking time: 2½–4 hours

Fish should never be overcooked. Fish dishes from the slow cooker will be juicy and tender, but note that cooking times are considerably shorter than for most other foods. If in doubt whether fish is done, lift the lid and test with a fork – the flesh should flake easily but still be moist. Be sure to allow for the thickness of the piece. Slashing the side of a whole fish at the thickest part will help it to cook evenly. Fish is usually best removed from the pot as soon as it is cooked.

opposite *Braised Guinea Fowl*
(page 32)

POULTRY AND GAME

Chicken is an ideal choice for the slow cooker — the result is tender, flavourful and moist. Bake it, stuff it, curry it, glaze it with orange or sweet and sour sauce — the variety is endless. And so is the range of additional ingredients, from lemon and bacon, sherry, olives, grapes and mustard to soup mixes, cider, vegetables, rice or tangy barbecue sauce.

The ease of cooking chicken in the pot is matched only by the taste of the finished dish, which your family will heartily applaud. Leftovers (if any) can of course be reheated in the slow cooker for another meal. Do remember, though, that frozen chicken should always be completely thawed in the refrigerator before cooking.

Pigeon and rabbit also make an appearance — cooked whole or in stews, the result will always be tender and moist. Try altering traditional family recipes to achieve an old-fashioned taste by modern methods. Any game will benefit from the intermingling of flavours produced through slow cooking.

Braised Guinea Fowl

METRIC/IMPERIAL
2 rashers bacon, rinded
1 guinea fowl, drawn and
   trussed
25 g/1 oz butter
1 tablespoon cooking oil
1 onion, chopped
0.5 kg/1 lb cabbage, shredded
300 ml/½ pint dry white wine
salt and pepper
sprigs of parsley and chopped
   walnuts to garnish

Secure the bacon rashers over the breast of the guinea fowl with cocktail sticks. Melt the butter and oil in a large frying pan and brown the fowl all over; lift out and put to one side. Fry the onion in the pan until soft but not brown. Blanch the cabbage, drain thoroughly and place with the onion in the slow cooker. Place the fowl on top.

Pour over the wine and season well. Cover and cook on HIGH for 30 minutes, then turn to LOW for 8–10 hours. Remove cocktail sticks and serve the guinea fowl on a bed of shredded cabbage. Garnish with sprigs of parsley and chopped walnuts.

AMERICAN
2 slices bacon, rinded
1 guinea fowl, drawn and
   trussed
2 tablespoons butter
1 tablespoon cooking oil
1 onion, chopped
3½ cups shredded cabbage
1¼ cups dry white wine
salt and pepper
sprigs of parsley and chopped
   walnuts to garnish

Serves 3
Slow cooking time: 8½–10½ hours

Orange Glazed Chicken

METRIC/IMPERIAL
50 g/2 oz brown sugar
1 tablespoon made mustard
salt and pepper
grated rind and juice of 2 large
   oranges
1.5-kg/3-lb roasting chicken
25 g/1 oz butter
15 g/½ oz cornflour
2 tablespoons water
orange slices and watercress to
   garnish (optional)

The oranges give a lovely flavour to the chicken. Serve with a green vegetable, such as beans or broccoli, and new potatoes.

Blend the sugar, mustard, salt and pepper with the orange rind and the juice, made up to 150 ml/¼ pint (US ⅔ cup) with water. Wipe the chicken, melt the butter in a pan and fry the chicken until brown on all sides. Lift out and place in the slow cooker. Add the orange mixture to the frying pan, bring to the boil and pour over the chicken. Cover and cook on HIGH for 3 hours.

Lift the chicken from the pot and place on a serving dish (if liked, it may be cut in portions). Keep warm.

Blend the cornflour with the water and stir into the pot; as the sauce is hot it will thicken at once. Cover and leave to cook for 5–10 minutes. Taste to check the seasoning and spoon the sauce over the chicken. If liked, garnish the dish with orange slices and watercress.

AMERICAN
¼ cup brown sugar
1 tablespoon prepared mustard
salt and pepper
grated rind and juice of 2 large
   oranges
3-lb roasting chicken
2 tablespoons butter
2 tablespoons cornstarch
3 tablespoons water
orange slices and watercress to
   garnish (optional)

Serves 4–6
Slow cooking time: 3¼ hours

Creamed Chicken Curry

METRIC/IMPERIAL
1.5-kg/3-lb chicken with giblets
1 small onion
2 whole cloves
2 small carrots, sliced
bay leaf
sprig parsley
1 teaspoon salt
pepper
300 ml/½ pint boiling water
25 g/1 oz butter
1 tablespoon curry powder
25 g/1 oz plain flour
100 g/4 oz green grapes
5 tablespoons double cream

Put the chicken with the giblets in the slow cooker and add the onion stuck with the cloves, the carrots, bay leaf, parsley and seasoning. Pour over the water, cover and cook on HIGH for 4–5 hours. Remove the chicken from the cooking liquid and leave to cool slightly. Strain the stock and keep on one side. Remove the flesh from the chicken and cut into neat slices or serving portions; arrange on a dish and keep warm.

Melt the butter in a pan, stir in the curry powder and cook gently for 2–3 minutes. Add the flour and cook for 1 minute. Skim any fat from the strained stock then add to the pan and bring to the boil, stirring until thickened. Halve the grapes and remove any pips. Stir into the sauce and taste to check the seasoning.

Remove the pan from the heat and stir in the cream. Spoon the sauce over the chicken and serve with plain boiled rice and a green salad.

AMERICAN
3-lb chicken with giblets
1 small onion
2 whole cloves
2 small carrots, sliced
bay leaf
sprig parsley
1 teaspoon salt
pepper
1¼ cups boiling water
2 tablespoons butter
1 tablespoon curry powder
¼ cup all-purpose flour
1 cup white grapes
6 tablespoons heavy cream

Serves 4–6
Slow cooking time: 4–5 hours

Chicken Fricassée

METRIC/IMPERIAL
1.5-kg/3-lb chicken with giblets
300 ml/½ pint boiling cider or water
sprig parsley
1 small onion, chopped
salt and pepper
1 small green pepper
1 small red pepper
40 g/1½ oz butter
1 large onion, chopped
40 g/1½ oz plain flour
150 ml/¼ pint milk

This dish freezes well. It may be used as a filling for pies or vol-au-vents or served on its own with creamed potatoes or rice and a green vegetable.

Place the chicken in the slow cooker with the giblets, cider or water, parsley, small onion and plenty of seasoning. Cover and cook on HIGH for 4–5 hours. Lift the chicken from the pot and leave to cool; strain off the stock. Remove the flesh from the chicken and cut into neat pieces.

Remove the seeds and white pith from the peppers and cut them into strips. Melt the butter in a pan and add the peppers and the large onion. Cover and cook gently without browning for 8–10 minutes. Stir in the flour. Cook for 2 minutes, stirring. Add the strained stock and bring to the boil, stirring well, and allow to thicken; simmer for 2 minutes. Stir the chicken pieces into the sauce with the milk. Heat through but do not boil. Taste to check the seasoning.

AMERICAN
3-lb chicken with giblets
1¼ cups boiling cider or water
sprig parsley
1 small onion, chopped
salt and pepper
1 small green pepper
1 small red pepper
3 tablespoons butter
1 large onion, chopped
6 tablespoons all-purpose flour
⅔ cup milk

Serves 6
Slow cooking time: 4–5 hours

Tilbury Chicken

METRIC/IMPERIAL
300 ml/½ pint cider
1.5-kg/3-lb chicken with
   giblets
1 onion, chopped
salt
freshly ground black pepper
milk
50 g/2 oz butter
50 g/2 oz plain flour
1 canned pimiento, sliced
12 stuffed green olives, sliced

Bring the cider to the boil in a saucepan. Put the chicken in the slow cooker with the giblets, onion, cider and seasoning. Cover and cook on HIGH for 4–5 hours. Lift the chicken out and leave to cool. Strain off the stock into a measure and make up to 750 ml/1¼ pints (US 1½ pints) with milk.

Remove the flesh from the chicken and cut into large pieces. Use the carcass and giblets later to make stock for soup (see page 16).

Melt the butter in a pan, add the flour and cook for 2 minutes; stir in the cider mixture and bring to the boil, stirring. Allow to thicken. Add the sliced pimiento and olives and season well. Stir in the chicken and allow to become piping hot, then turn into a dish and serve with plain boiled rice.

AMERICAN
1¼ cups cider
3-lb chicken with giblets
1 onion, chopped
salt
freshly ground black pepper
milk
¼ cup butter
½ cup all-purpose flour
1 canned pimiento, sliced
12 stuffed green olives, sliced

Serves 6
Slow cooking time: 4–5 hours

Sweet and Sour Chicken

METRIC/IMPERIAL
2 tablespoons cooking oil
4 chicken joints
25 g/1 oz plain flour
283-g/10-oz can pineapple
   pieces
2 tablespoons soya sauce
1 tablespoon sherry
2 pieces stem ginger, finely
   chopped
salt and pepper

Heat the oil in a frying pan and fry the chicken joints until golden brown. Lift out and place in the slow cooker. Blend the flour with the oil remaining in the pan and cook for 1 minute. Drain the juice from the pineapple and make up to 300 ml/½ pint (US 1¼ cups) with water; add to the pan and bring to the boil, stirring until thickened. Add the remaining ingredients including the pineapple pieces, mix well and return to the boil. Pour over the chicken, cover and cook on HIGH for 30 minutes then turn to LOW for 4 hours. Serve with ribbon noodles or rice and a green salad.

AMERICAN
3 tablespoons cooking oil
4 chicken joints
¼ cup all-purpose flour
10-oz can pineapple chunks
3 tablespoons soy sauce
1 tablespoon sherry
2 pieces preserved ginger,
   finely chopped
salt and pepper

Serves 4
Slow cooking time: 4½ hours

Tetley Chicken

METRIC/IMPERIAL
1 tablespoon cooking oil
4 chicken joints
4 tablespoons bottled
   Thousand Island dressing
100 g/4 oz apricot jam
½ packet French onion soup mix
1 clove garlic, crushed
1 tablespoon Dijon mustard

A quick and easy dish to prepare. Serve with a green salad and chunks of French bread.

Heat the oil in a frying pan and quickly brown the chicken joints. Combine the rest of the ingredients, then lift the chicken out and place in the slow cooker. Add the sauce to the pan and bring to the boil, stirring. Pour over the chicken, cover the pot and cook on HIGH for 3 hours.

AMERICAN
1 tablespoon cooking oil
4 chicken joints
⅓ cup Thousand Island dressing
⅓ cup apricot jam
½ package French onion soup
   mix
1 clove garlic, crushed
1 tablespoon Dijon mustard

Serves 4
Slow cooking time: 3 hours

opposite *Tilbury Chicken*

Baked Chicken with Lemon and Bacon

METRIC/IMPERIAL
4 chicken joints
2 tablespoons cooking oil
225 g/8 oz tomatoes
juice of 1 lemon
salt
freshly ground black pepper
4 rashers streaky bacon
chopped parsley to garnish

This is a very simple way of cooking chicken, while the lemon and bacon give it a marvellous flavour.

Remove the skin from the chicken joints. Heat the oil in a frying pan, add the chicken and fry lightly to brown. Peel the tomatoes, slice thickly and lay them in the bottom of the slow cooker. Place the chicken on top, spoon over the lemon juice and season well.

Cut the rind from the bacon and lay a rasher over each chicken joint, cover the pot and cook on HIGH for 30 minutes, then turn to LOW and cook for a further $3\frac{1}{2}$–4 hours.

Place the chicken on a serving dish, spoon the sauce and tomatoes over and sprinkle with parsley. Serve with new potatoes and broccoli or green beans.

Serves 4
Slow cooking time: 4–4$\frac{1}{2}$ hours

AMERICAN
4 chicken joints
3 tablespoons cooking oil
$\frac{1}{2}$ lb tomatoes
juice of 1 lemon
salt
freshly ground black pepper
4 slices bacon
chopped parsley to garnish

Sunday Pot Roast Chicken

METRIC/IMPERIAL
Stuffing:
25 g/1 oz butter
1 chicken liver
1 small onion, finely chopped
175 g/6 oz pork sausagemeat
100 g/4 oz fresh white
    breadcrumbs
1 tablespoon chopped parsley
$\frac{1}{4}$ teaspoon dried thyme
grated rind and juice of $\frac{1}{2}$ lemon
$\frac{1}{2}$ teaspoon salt
pinch freshly ground black
    pepper
$\frac{1}{2}$ beaten egg

1.5-kg/3$\frac{1}{4}$-lb frozen chicken,
    defrosted
25 g/1 oz butter
1 tablespoon cooking oil
3–4 sticks celery, sliced
225 g/8 oz carrots, peeled and
    sliced
175 g/6 oz leeks, washed and
    sliced
$\frac{1}{2}$ teaspoon salt
freshly ground black pepper
150 ml/$\frac{1}{4}$ pint chicken stock

Make the stuffing: melt the butter in a small pan, add the chicken liver and onion and fry for 5 minutes, stirring. Add all the remaining stuffing ingredients and mix well. Stuff the neck end of the chicken and truss securely.

Melt the butter and oil in a frying pan and fry the chicken, browning on all sides. Remove from pan and put on one side. Fry the vegetables in the fat remaining in the pan, season and add the stock. Bring to the boil and put in the slow cooker. Lay the stuffed chicken on top, cover and cook on HIGH for $3\frac{1}{2}$–4 hours.

Serves 6
Slow cooking time: 3$\frac{1}{2}$–4 hours

AMERICAN
Stuffing:
2 tablespoons butter
1 chicken liver
1 small onion, finely chopped
$\frac{3}{4}$ cup pork sausagemeat
2 cups fresh white bread
    crumbs
1 tablespoon chopped parsley
$\frac{1}{4}$ teaspoon dried thyme
grated rind and juice of $\frac{1}{2}$ lemon
$\frac{1}{2}$ teaspoon salt
pinch freshly ground black
    pepper
$\frac{1}{2}$ beaten egg

3$\frac{1}{4}$-lb frozen chicken,
    defrosted
2 tablespoons butter
1 tablespoon cooking oil
3–4 stalks celery, sliced
$\frac{1}{2}$ lb carrots, peeled and sliced
6 oz leeks, washed and sliced
$\frac{1}{2}$ teaspoon salt
freshly ground black pepper
$\frac{2}{3}$ cup chicken stock

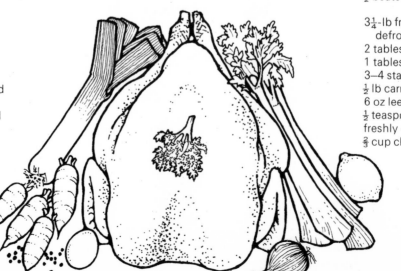

Chicken with Orange and Watercress Stuffing

METRIC/IMPERIAL
Stuffing:
finely grated rind of ½ orange
75 g/3 oz fresh white
    breadcrumbs
½ bunch watercress, chopped
chicken stock cube, crumbled
1 egg, beaten

1.5-kg/3¼-lb oven-ready
    chicken
2 tablespoons cooking oil
1 large onion, chopped
½ head celery, chopped
150 ml/¼ pint chicken stock
juice of ½ orange
salt and pepper
25 g/1 oz walnuts
1 tablespoon chopped parsley

Mix all the stuffing ingredients together and stuff into the neck end of the chicken. Heat the oil in a frying pan and fry the chicken until golden brown all over; lift out and put on one side. Add the vegetables to the pan and fry for 3–4 minutes without browning.

Add the chicken stock and orange juice and bring to the boil. Turn into the slow cooker, put the chicken on top and season. Cover and cook on HIGH for 3½–4 hours. Stir in the walnuts and parsley and taste to check the seasoning. Place the chicken on a serving dish and spoon the vegetables and sauce round.

Serves 6
Slow cooking time: 3½–4 hours

AMERICAN
Stuffing:
finely grated rind of ½ orange
1½ cups fresh white bread
    crumbs
½ bunch watercress, chopped
chicken bouillon cube,
    crumbled
1 egg, beaten

3¼-lb oven-ready chicken
3 tablespoons cooking oil
1 large onion, chopped
½ bunch celery, chopped
⅔ cup chicken stock
juice of ½ orange
salt and pepper
¼ cup walnuts
1 tablespoon chopped parsley

Chicken with Olives

METRIC/IMPERIAL
4 chicken joints
25 g/1 oz plain flour
50 g/2 oz butter
2 large onions, chopped
1 large red pepper
150 ml/¼ pint chicken stock or
    water
227-g/8-oz can tomatoes
1 teaspoon salt
freshly ground black pepper
25 g/1 oz stuffed green olives,
    sliced

Coat the chicken joints in the flour. Melt the butter in a frying pan and fry the chicken until golden brown, lift out and place in the slow cooker. Add the onions to the butter remaining in the pan and fry for 2–3 minutes.

Remove the seeds and white pith from the pepper and slice it into rings. Add the remaining ingredients to the pan, except for the olives, and bring to the boil.

Pour over the chicken joints and cover. Cook on HIGH for 30 minutes, then turn to LOW for a further 3½ hours. Add the olives to the pot and cook for a further 30 minutes. Taste to check the seasoning before serving the chicken garnished with pepper rings. Hand the sauce separately, with saffron rice.

Serves 4
Slow cooking time: 4½ hours

AMERICAN
4 chicken joints
¼ cup all-purpose flour
¼ cup butter
2 large onions, chopped
1 large red pepper
⅔ cup chicken stock or water
8-oz can tomatoes
1 teaspoon salt
freshly ground black pepper
3 tablespoons stuffed green
    olives, sliced

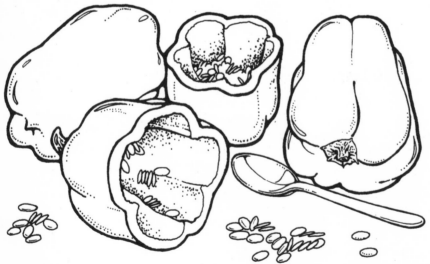

opposite *Sunday Pot Roast Chicken (page 36)*

above *Chicken with Olives (page 37)*

Summer Chicken Casserole

METRIC/IMPERIAL
50 g/2 oz butter
4 chicken joints
2 onions, chopped
1 clove garlic, crushed
40 g/1½ oz plain flour
300 ml/½ pint chicken stock
4 sticks celery, sliced
2 carrots, peeled and sliced
1 green pepper, cut in strips
½ teaspoon salt
freshly ground black pepper
225 g/8 oz small tomatoes

Melt the butter in a frying pan. Fry the chicken joints until brown on both sides, lift out and place in the slow cooker. Add the onions and garlic to the pan and fry for 2–3 minutes. Add the flour and cook for a further 1 minute, stir in the stock and bring to the boil. Simmer until thickened.

Add the celery, carrots and green pepper to the sauce, return to the boil and add the seasoning. Pour the sauce over the chicken joints, cover and cook on HIGH for 30 minutes, then turn to LOW and cook for a further 4–5 hours.

Peel the tomatoes, add them to the pot and cook for a further 30 minutes. Serve over rice or noodles.

AMERICAN
¼ cup butter
4 chicken joints
2 onions, chopped
1 clove garlic, crushed
6 tablespoons all-purpose flour
1¼ cups chicken stock
4 stalks celery, sliced
2 carrots, peeled and sliced
1 green pepper, cut in strips
½ teaspoon salt
freshly ground black pepper
½ lb small tomatoes

Serves 4
Slow cooking time: 5–6 hours

Poacher's Pot

METRIC/IMPERIAL
1 small rabbit, jointed
50 g/2 oz dripping
2 onions, chopped
2 large carrots, peeled and
    finely sliced
2 potatoes, finely sliced
25 g/1 oz plain flour
300 ml/½ pint stock
¼ teaspoon mixed dried herbs
1 teaspoon salt
freshly ground black pepper

Thoroughly wash and dry the rabbit. Heat the dripping in a large frying pan and fry the rabbit until golden brown; lift out and put in the slow cooker. Add the onions, carrots and potatoes to the fat remaining in the pan and fry for 3–4 minutes. Stir in the flour and cook for a further 1 minute. Add the stock and bring to the boil, stirring until the sauce has thickened, then add the herbs and seasoning.

Pour over the rabbit, cover and cook on HIGH for 30 minutes, then turn to LOW and cook for a further 6 hours.

AMERICAN
1 small rabbit, jointed
¼ cup drippings
2 onions, chopped
2 large carrots, peeled and
    finely sliced
2 potatoes, finely sliced
¼ cup all-purpose flour
1¼ cups stock
¼ teaspoon mixed dried herbs
1 teaspoon salt
freshly ground black pepper

Serves 6
Slow cooking time: 6½ hours

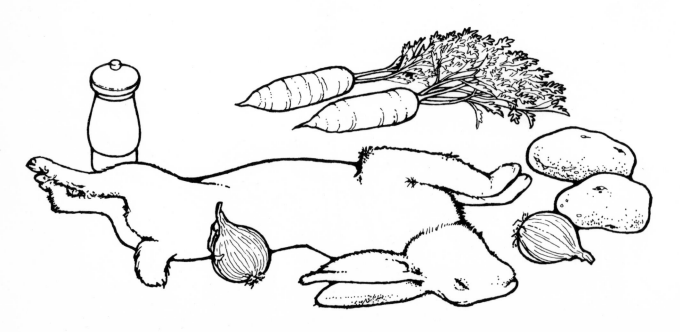

Southern Chicken

METRIC/IMPERIAL
4 chicken joints
25 g/1 oz plain flour
3 tablespoons cooking oil
1 small green pepper, sliced
225 g/8 oz new carrots, finely sliced
227-g/8-oz can pineapple pieces
297-g/10½-oz can condensed tomato soup
salt and pepper

Remove the skin from the chicken and coat in the flour. Heat the oil in a frying pan and fry the chicken joints until golden brown. Lift out and place in the slow cooker. Add the sliced green pepper and carrots to the oil remaining in the pan and fry for 5 minutes. Stir in any remaining flour, the syrup drained from the can of pineapple and the can of soup and bring to the boil, stirring. Add seasoning to taste, pour the sauce over the chicken, cover and cook on HIGH for 30 minutes, then turn to LOW and cook for a further 3½–4 hours. Add the pineapple pieces for the last 1 hour of the cooking time.

AMERICAN
4 chicken joints
¼ cup all-purpose flour
¼ cup cooking oil
1 small green pepper, sliced
½ lb new carrots, finely sliced
8-oz can pineapple chunks
10½-oz can condensed tomato soup
salt and pepper

Serves 4
Slow cooking time: 4–4½ hours

American Style Chicken

METRIC/IMPERIAL
salt and pepper
4 chicken joints
1 tablespoon cooking oil
Barbecue sauce:
2 tablespoons wine vinegar
1 tablespoon soya sauce
15 g/½ oz cornflour
1 tablespoon Worcestershire sauce
2 teaspoons castor sugar
2 tablespoons tomato ketchup
2 cloves garlic, crushed
dash Tabasco sauce
4 tablespoons water

A very easy dish to prepare. The tasty barbecue sauce can also be used for pork or sliced beef. Serve the chicken with ribbon noodles, sprinkled with chopped parsley.

Season the chicken joints. Heat the oil in a frying pan and fry the chicken quickly until brown, then lift out and place in the slow cooker.

Blend all the sauce ingredients together and pour into the frying pan; bring to the boil, stirring until thickened, and pour over the chicken. Cover and cook on HIGH for 30 minutes then turn to LOW and cook for a further 4 hours or until the chicken is tender.

AMERICAN
salt and pepper
4 chicken joints
1 tablespoon cooking oil
Barbecue sauce:
3 tablespoons wine vinegar
1 tablespoon soy sauce
2 tablespoons cornstarch
1 tablespoon Worcestershire sauce
2 teaspoons sugar
3 tablespoons tomato ketchup
2 cloves garlic, crushed
dash Tabasco sauce
⅓ cup water

Serves 4
Slow cooking time: 4½ hours

Chicken Risotto

METRIC/IMPERIAL
2 tablespoons cooking oil
1 onion, chopped
225 g/8 oz long-grain rice
1 clove garlic, crushed
pinch turmeric
750 ml/1¼ pints chicken stock
1 green pepper, seeded and chopped
1 teaspoon salt
225 g/8 oz cooked chicken, diced
100 g/4 oz mushrooms, sliced
4 tomatoes, skinned and quartered

Heat the oil in a pan and fry the onion for 3–4 minutes, without browning. Add the raw rice and garlic and fry until all the oil is absorbed. Stir in the turmeric, stock, chopped green pepper and salt and bring to the boil, stirring.

Turn into the slow cooker, cover and cook on LOW for 3–4 hours. (The cooking time will vary with the type of rice and the size of the pot.)

Add the chicken, mushrooms and tomatoes, stir lightly with a fork and cook for a further 30 minutes. Taste to check the seasoning and serve with a green salad.

Serves 4
Slow cooking time : 3½–4½ hours

AMERICAN
3 tablespoons cooking oil
1 onion, chopped
1 cup long-grain rice
1 clove garlic, crushed
pinch turmeric
1½ pints chicken stock
1 green pepper, seeded and chopped
1 teaspoon salt
1 cup diced cooked chicken
1 cup mushrooms, sliced
4 tomatoes, skinned and quartered

Pigeon Normandy

METRIC/IMPERIAL
2 pigeons, split
25 g/1 oz plain flour
50 g/2 oz butter
2 small onions, chopped
2 sticks celery, sliced
300 ml/½ pint dry cider
2 apples, peeled, cored and sliced
salt and pepper
3 tablespoons double cream

Cider is far more suitable for combining with apples in this dish than the usual white wine.

Wipe the pigeons and coat with flour. Melt the butter in a pan and fry the pigeons until golden brown. Lift out and place in the slow cooker. Add the onions and celery to the pan, cover and cook for 5 minutes. Add any remaining flour to the pan and cook gently until starting to brown. Add the cider and bring to the boil, stirring until thickened.

Add the apples and seasoning to the sauce and pour over the pigeons. Cover the pot and cook on HIGH for 30 minutes, then turn to LOW and cook for a further 4 hours or until tender.

Lift out the pigeons and arrange on a serving dish. Stir the cream into the sauce in the pot and spoon over the pigeons; serve at once.

Serves 4
Slow cooking time : 4½ hours

AMERICAN
2 pigeons, split
¼ cup all-purpose flour
¼ cup butter
2 small onions, chopped
2 stalks celery, sliced
1¼ cups dry cider
2 apples, peeled, cored and sliced
salt and pepper
¼ cup heavy cream

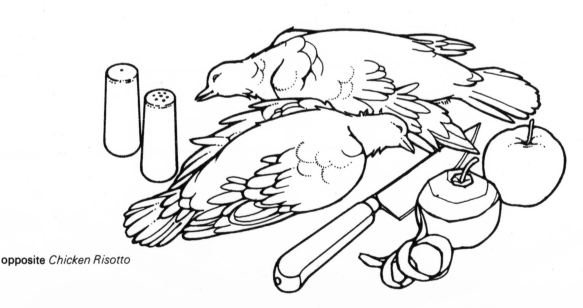

opposite *Chicken Risotto*

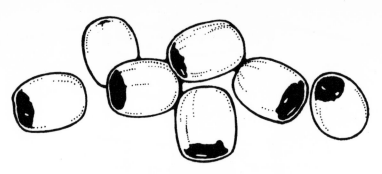

Chicken in Sherry Sauce

METRIC/IMPERIAL
3 tablespoons cooking oil
4 chicken joints
2 large onions, sliced
2 cloves garlic, crushed
25 g/1 oz plain flour
397-g/14-oz can tomatoes
150 ml/¼ pint chicken stock
salt and pepper
3—4 tablespoons sherry
12 stuffed green olives, sliced
1 canned pimiento,
   sliced, to garnish

AMERICAN
¼ cup cooking oil
4 chicken joints
2 large onions, sliced
2 cloves garlic, crushed
¼ cup all-purpose flour
14-oz can tomatoes
⅔ cup chicken stock
salt and pepper
¼—⅓ cup sherry
12 stuffed green olives, sliced
1 canned pimiento, sliced, to
   garnish

Heat the oil in a frying pan and fry the chicken joints until golden brown. Lift out and place in the slow cooker. Add the onions and garlic to the oil and fry without browning for 2—3 minutes. Stir in the flour and cook for 1 minute, then add the tomatoes and stock and bring to the boil. Season well and pour over the chicken, cover and cook on HIGH for 30 minutes then turn to LOW for 4 hours.

Lift out the chicken and put on one side. Reduce the sauce to a purée in a liquidiser or put through a sieve and return to the pot with the sherry and olives; check the seasoning. Add the chicken joints, cover and heat through on HIGH for 30 minutes. Garnish with slices of pimiento and serve with saffron rice.

Serves 4
Slow cooking time: 5 hours

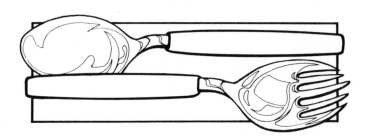

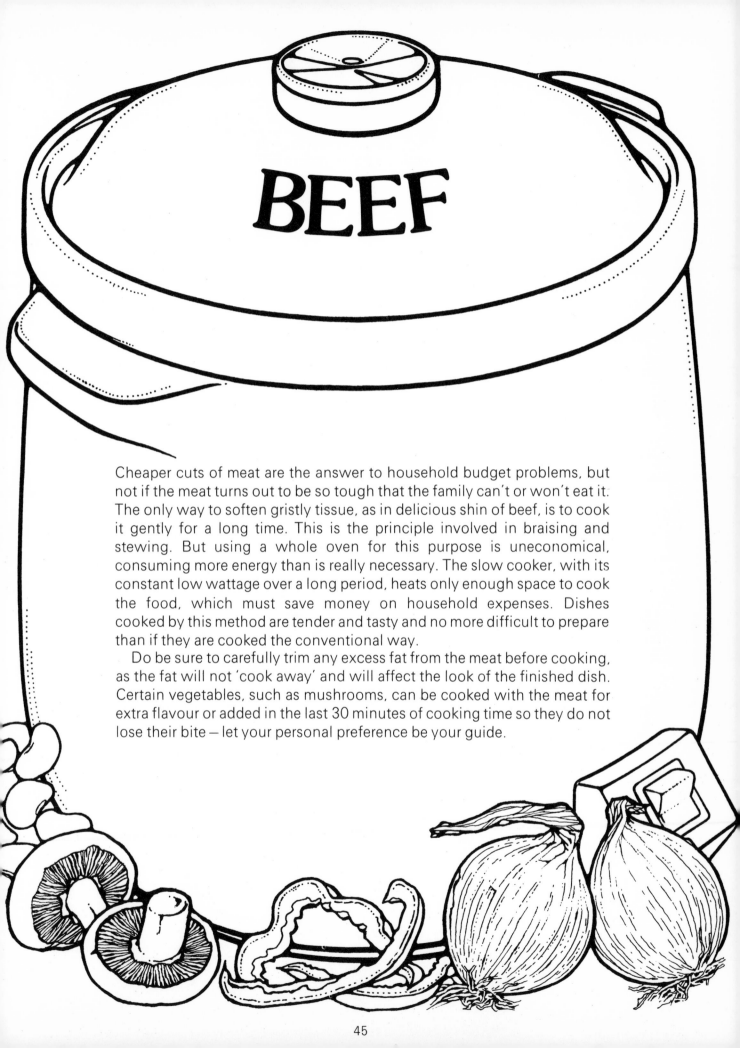

BEEF

Cheaper cuts of meat are the answer to household budget problems, but not if the meat turns out to be so tough that the family can't or won't eat it. The only way to soften gristly tissue, as in delicious shin of beef, is to cook it gently for a long time. This is the principle involved in braising and stewing. But using a whole oven for this purpose is uneconomical, consuming more energy than is really necessary. The slow cooker, with its constant low wattage over a long period, heats only enough space to cook the food, which must save money on household expenses. Dishes cooked by this method are tender and tasty and no more difficult to prepare than if they are cooked the conventional way.

Do be sure to carefully trim any excess fat from the meat before cooking, as the fat will not 'cook away' and will affect the look of the finished dish. Certain vegetables, such as mushrooms, can be cooked with the meat for extra flavour or added in the last 30 minutes of cooking time so they do not lose their bite — let your personal preference be your guide.

Boeuf Français

METRIC/IMPERIAL
1 kg/2 lb topside of beef, cut in
   3.5-cm/1½-inch pieces
25 g/1 oz plain flour
1 teaspoon salt
¼ teaspoon pepper
2 tablespoons cooking oil
25 g/1 oz butter
100 g/4 oz salt pork
2 onions, chopped
1 clove garlic, crushed
bay leaf
sprig thyme
sprig parsley
150 ml/¼ pint stock
300 ml/½ pint red wine
100 g/4 oz button mushrooms
4 tablespoons brandy

Put the beef cubes in a paper or polythene bag with the flour and seasoning and toss well. Heat the oil with the butter in a frying pan. Remove the rind and bones from the salt pork, cut in strips and fry until crisp and brown. Lift out and put the pork strips in the slow cooker. Fry the beef, onions and garlic in the pan until brown, lift out and add to the pot. Add the herbs, stock and wine to the pan, bring to the boil and pour over the beef.

Cover and cook on HIGH for 30 minutes, then turn to LOW for 4 hours. Add the whole mushrooms and brandy and cook for a further 30 minutes. Remove herbs before serving with buttered noodles or new potatoes and a crisp green salad.

Serves 8
Slow cooking time: 5 hours

AMERICAN
2 lb top round of beef, cut in
   1½-inch pieces
¼ cup all-purpose flour
1 teaspoon salt
¼ teaspoon pepper
3 tablespoons cooking oil
2 tablespoons butter
¼ lb salt pork
2 onions, chopped
1 clove garlic, crushed
bay leaf
sprig thyme
sprig parsley
⅔ cup stock
1¼ cups red wine
1 cup button mushrooms
⅓ cup brandy

Steak and Kidney Pudding

METRIC/IMPERIAL
0.5 kg/1 lb stewing steak
100 g/4 oz ox kidney
25 g/1 oz plain flour
1 small onion, finely chopped
salt and pepper
150 ml/¼ pint stock (approx.)
boiling water
Suet pastry:
225 g/8 oz self-raising flour
1 teaspoon salt
100 g/4 oz shredded suet
150 ml/¼ pint cold water
   (approx.)

Grease a generous litre/2-pint (US 2½-pint) pudding basin. Cut the steak into 1-cm/½-inch cubes, remove the skin and core from the kidney and cut it into small pieces. Toss in the flour with the onion and seasoning.

Now prepare the pastry: put the flour, salt and suet in a bowl and mix with sufficient water to make a soft but not sticky dough. Cut off a third of the dough and roll out to a circle the size of the top of the basin to make a lid. Roll out the remainder and line the basin with it. Fill the basin with the meat mixture and add sufficient stock to come three quarters of the way up the meat. Damp the edges of the pastry and cover with the lid, sealing firmly.

Cover the pudding with a piece of greased greaseproof paper and a lid of pleated foil. Stand the basin on a jam jar lid in the slow cooker and pour in sufficient boiling water to come halfway up the sides of the basin. Cover and cook on HIGH for 5 hours. Lift out of the pot and remove the foil and greaseproof paper lids. Run a knife carefully round the edge of the pudding and turn out on to a serving dish.

Serves 4–6
Slow cooking time: 5 hours

AMERICAN
1 lb flank meat
¼ lb beef kidney
¼ cup all-purpose flour
1 small onion, finely chopped
salt and pepper
⅔ cup stock (approx.)
boiling water
Suet pastry:
2 cups all-purpose flour sifted
   with 2 teaspoons baking
   powder
1 teaspoon salt
⅔ cup chopped suet
⅔ cup cold water (approx.)

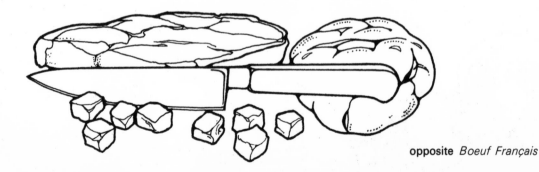

opposite *Boeuf Français*

Steak, Kidney and Mushroom Casserole

METRIC/IMPERIAL
0.5 kg/1 lb skirt of beef, cut in
   2.5-cm/1-inch cubes
225 g/8 oz ox kidney, cut in
   1-cm/½-inch cubes
25 g/1 oz plain flour
25 g/1 oz dripping
1 large onion, sliced
300 ml/½ pint beef stock
bay leaf
100 g/4 oz mushrooms, sliced
1 teaspoon salt
freshly ground black pepper

If you are using a large pot, double up on this recipe – then eat half and freeze half.

Coat the cubes of steak and kidney in flour. Melt the dripping in a frying pan and fry the meat and onion until brown, then transfer the meat to the slow cooker using a slotted spoon. Add the remaining ingredients to the pan and bring to the boil. Pour over the meat, cover and cook on HIGH for 30 minutes then turn to LOW for 7–8 hours. Remove the bay leaf and check the seasoning before serving.

Serves 4–6
Slow cooking time: 7½–8½ hours

AMERICAN
1 lb beef chuck, cut in
   1-inch cubes
½ lb beef kidney, cut in
   ½-inch cubes
¼ cup all-purpose flour
2 tablespoons drippings
1 large onion, sliced
1¼ cups beef stock
bay leaf
1 cup sliced mushrooms
1 teaspoon salt
freshly ground black pepper

Canterbury Steak

METRIC/IMPERIAL
6 (100-g/4-oz) slices braising
   steak
25 g/1 oz seasoned plain flour
40 g/1½ oz dripping
2 onions, sliced
2 sticks celery, sliced
397-g/14-oz can tomatoes
1 teaspoon Worcestershire
   sauce
150 ml/¼ pint water
salt and pepper

This recipe is for six people, but it would be easy to adapt for any number to suit your family and your slow cooker.

Coat the meat in the seasoned flour. Melt the dripping in a frying pan and fry the meat quickly on both sides to brown. Transfer the meat to the slow cooker. Add the onions and celery to the fat remaining in the pan and fry until pale golden brown. Lift out and put in the pot.

Add the tomatoes, Worcestershire sauce and water to the pan, bring to the boil and season well. Pour over the meat and vegetables, cover and cook on HIGH for 30 minutes then turn to LOW and cook for a further 5 hours.

Serves 6
Slow cooking time: 5½ hours

AMERICAN
6 (¼-lb) slices flank steak
¼ cup seasoned all-purpose
   flour
3 tablespoons drippings
2 onions, sliced
2 stalks celery, sliced
14-oz can tomatoes
1 teaspoon Worcestershire
   sauce
⅔ cup water
salt and pepper

Spiced Salt Beef

METRIC/IMPERIAL
1.5 kg/3 lb salt brisket or
   silverside of beef
2 onions, sliced
2 carrots, peeled and sliced
2 bay leaves
1 clove garlic, peeled
6 peppercorns
1 teaspoon ground ginger
600 ml/1 pint boiling dry cider

Put the beef into a large bowl, cover with cold water and leave to soak for 2 hours. Drain and place in the slow cooker with all the other ingredients. Cover and cook on HIGH for 1 hour then turn to LOW for 8 hours.

Lift the beef from the pot, wrap in greaseproof paper and put in a cake tin or soufflé dish that will fit the joint snugly. Cover with a plate and a heavy weight, cool then chill in the refrigerator for 24 hours. Unwrap the beef, carve into thin slices and serve with a selection of salads.

Serves 8
Slow cooking time: 9 hours

AMERICAN
3 lb corned beef brisket
2 onions, sliced
2 carrots, peeled and sliced
2 bay leaves
1 clove garlic, peeled
6 peppercorns
1 teaspoon ground ginger
2½ cups boiling dry cider

Braised Beef in Beer

METRIC/IMPERIAL
1¼ lb chuck steak
225 g/8 oz onions, sliced
2 carrots, peeled and sliced
300 ml/½ pint light ale
40 g/1½ oz plain flour
40 g/1½ oz dripping
1 tablespoon brown sugar
1½ teaspoons French mustard
1 teaspoon salt
freshly ground black pepper

Cut the beef into four steaks, about 1 cm/½ inch thick and 10 cm/4 inches across, and put in an earthenware dish with the onions and carrots. Pour over the ale and leave to stand for 24 hours.

Remove the meat from the marinade and coat each piece in the flour. Melt the dripping in a frying pan, fry the meat until brown on both sides and place in the slow cooker. Add the vegetables and marinade to the pan along with the remaining ingredients and bring to the boil. Pour over the meat, cover and cook on HIGH for 30 minutes then on LOW for about 6 hours. Serve with a green vegetable or crisp salad.

AMERICAN
1¼ lb chuck steak
½ lb onions, sliced
2 carrots, peeled and sliced
1¼ cups ale or beer
⅓ cup all-purpose flour
3 tablespoons drippings
1 tablespoon brown sugar
1½ teaspoons French mustard
1 teaspoon salt
freshly ground black pepper

Serves 4
Slow cooking time: 6½ hours

Beef Stroganoff

METRIC/IMPERIAL
0.75 kg/1½ lb chuck steak
75 g/3 oz butter
1 large onion, chopped
100 g/4 oz button mushrooms, sliced
225 g/8 oz tomatoes, peeled, quartered and seeded
1 tablespoon cooking oil
salt and pepper
2 (150-ml/5-oz) cartons soured cream
sprigs parsley or watercress to garnish

Gone is the time when I could afford fillet or rump steak for this recipe. I find chuck steak is different and equally delicious.

Cut the steak into strips 5 cm/2 inches long, 1 cm/½ inch wide and 5 mm/¼ inch thick. Melt two thirds of the butter in a frying pan and fry the onion slowly until soft; lift out with a slotted spoon and place in the slow cooker. Add the mushrooms and tomatoes to the pan and fry for 2–3 minutes, lift out and add to the pot. Add the remaining butter and the oil to the pan and fry the steak for 2–3 minutes. Add the steak to the pot, season well, cover and cook on HIGH for 3 hours or until tender. Unplug the pot, remove the lid and stir in the soured cream just before serving. Garnish with small sprigs of parsley or watercress.

AMERICAN
1½ lb chuck steak
⅓ cup butter
1 large onion, chopped
1 cup sliced button mushrooms
½ lb tomatoes, peeled, quartered and seeded
1 tablespoon cooking oil
salt and pepper
2 (5-oz) cartons dairy sour cream
sprigs parsley or watercress to garnish

Serves 6
Slow cooking time: 3 hours

Boiled Salt Beef with Mustard Sauce (page 52)

Boiled Salt Beef with Mustard Sauce

METRIC/IMPERIAL
1.25 kg/2½ lb salted silverside or brisket of beef
1 onion, sliced
1 parsnip, sliced
2 carrots, peeled and sliced
boiling water
freshly ground black pepper
Dumplings:
100 g/4 oz self-raising flour
50 g/2 oz shredded suet
salt and pepper
6 tablespoons water (approx.)
Mustard sauce:
25 g/1 oz margarine
25 g/1 oz plain flour
150 ml/¼ pint milk
150 ml/¼ pint meat stock
2 tablespoons cider vinegar
1 tablespoon sugar
1½ teaspoons dry mustard

Soak the silverside overnight to remove the excess salt, drain and put it in the slow cooker with the vegetables round it. Add sufficient boiling water to just cover the meat and season with plenty of black pepper.

Cover the pot and cook on HIGH for 1 hour then on LOW for 7 hours.

Turn the slow cooker to HIGH and make the dumplings: mix the flour, suet and seasoning together and add sufficient water to make a firm dough. Shape the dough into eight equal pieces and drop into the pot, cover and cook on HIGH for 40 minutes. Lift out the meat, vegetables and dumplings with a slotted spoon, arrange on a serving dish and keep warm.

To make the mustard sauce: melt the margarine in a saucepan, add the flour and cook for 1 minute. Add the milk and measured stock from the pot and bring to the boil, stirring. Blend the vinegar, sugar and mustard together and stir into the sauce. Bring to the boil and simmer for 2–3 minutes. Taste to check the seasoning and serve with the silverside, vegetables and dumplings.

AMERICAN
2½ lb corned beef brisket
1 onion, sliced
1 parsnip, sliced
2 carrots, peeled and sliced
boiling water
freshly ground black pepper
Dumplings:
1 cup all-purpose flour sifted with 1 teaspoon baking powder
⅓ cup chopped suet
salt and pepper
½ cup water (approx.)
Mustard sauce:
2 tablespoons margarine
¼ cup all-purpose flour
⅔ cup milk
⅔ cup meat stock
3 tablespoons cider vinegar
1 tablespoon sugar
1½ teaspoons dry mustard

Serves 8
Slow cooking time: 8¾ hours

Spiced Beef and Beans

METRIC/IMPERIAL
0.5 kg/1 lb braising steak
½ teaspoon salt
freshly ground black pepper
15 g/½ oz dripping
15 g/½ oz plain flour
rind and juice of 1 large orange
2 tablespoons tomato ketchup
2 tablespoons malt vinegar
1 tablespoon Worcestershire sauce
dash Tabasco sauce
425-g/15-oz can kidney beans
orange wedges to garnish (optional)

Cut the meat into 2.5-cm/1-inch cubes and season well. Melt the dripping in a frying pan and quickly fry the steak to brown, lift out with a slotted spoon and place in the slow cooker. Stir the flour into the fat remaining in the pan and add the orange rind and juice, ketchup, vinegar, Worcestershire sauce and Tabasco. Cook until thickened then spoon over the meat, cover and cook on HIGH for 30 minutes then on LOW for 5 hours.

Drain the kidney beans, stir the beans into the pot and cook on LOW for a further 1 hour. Taste to check the seasoning (it may be necessary to add a little sugar). Turn on to a serving dish and if liked garnish with wedges of orange.

AMERICAN
1 lb flank steak
½ teaspoon salt
freshly ground black pepper
1 tablespoon drippings
2 tablespoons all-purpose flour
rind and juice of 1 large orange
3 tablespoons tomato ketchup
3 tablespoons malt vinegar
1 tablespoon Worcestershire sauce
dash Tabasco sauce
15-oz can kidney beans
orange wedges to garnish (optional)

Serves 4
Slow cooking time: 6½ hours

Devilled Beef

METRIC/IMPERIAL
0.75 kg/1½ lb stewing steak
25 g/1 oz dripping
225 g/8 oz onions, sliced
1 clove garlic, crushed
25 g/1 oz plain flour
2 teaspoons made mustard
397-g/14-oz can tomatoes
1 tablespoon chutney
1 tablespoon honey
salt and pepper

Cut the stewing steak in 2.5-cm/1-inch cubes. Melt the dripping in a frying pan and fry the steak, onions and garlic until brown. Lift out with a slotted spoon and place in the slow cooker. Stir the flour into the fat remaining in the pan and cook for 1 minute. Stir in the remaining ingredients and bring to the boil. Pour over the meat, cover the pot and cook on HIGH for 30 minutes, then turn to LOW for 6–7 hours.

Serves 4–6
Slow cooking time: 6½–7½ hours

AMERICAN
1½ lb flank meat
2 tablespoons drippings
½ lb onions, sliced
1 clove garlic, crushed
¼ cup all-purpose flour
2 teaspoons prepared mustard
14-oz can tomatoes
1 tablespoon chutney
1 tablespoon honey
salt and pepper

Beef and Potato Braise

METRIC/IMPERIAL
4 (100-g/4-oz) slices braising steak
2 tablespoons cooking oil
2 onions, sliced
0.5 kg/1¼ lb potatoes, thinly sliced
300 ml/½ pint stock
salt
freshly ground black pepper
225 g/8 oz tomatoes, peeled

This is a very good dish to leave for the family when you will not be back at mealtime as it is complete in itself. Leave the tomatoes ready on the side to be popped in just before serving.

Trim any excess fat from the steak. Heat the oil in a frying pan and fry the meat quickly for 2–3 minutes to brown both sides. Lift out and put in the slow cooker. Add the onions to the pan and fry for 3–4 minutes then add the potatoes and stock and bring to the boil. Pour over the meat and season well. Cover the pot and cook on HIGH for 30 minutes then turn to LOW for 7 hours. Add the tomatoes, cut in quarters, for the last 15 minutes of the cooking time.

Serves 4
Slow cooking time: 7½ hours

AMERICAN
4 (¼-lb) slices flank steak
3 tablespoons cooking oil
2 onions, sliced
1¼ lb potatoes, thinly sliced
1¼ cups stock
salt
freshly ground black pepper
½ lb tomatoes, peeled

Italian Parcels

METRIC/IMPERIAL
Filling:
1 small onion, chopped
0.5 kg/1 lb lean minced beef
½ teaspoon mixed dried herbs
1 teaspoon salt
¼ teaspoon pepper
150 ml/¼ pint beef stock
50 g/2 oz cooked rice

12 cabbage leaves
397-g/14-oz can tomatoes
salt and pepper

Place the onion and minced beef in a frying pan and cook until brown; add the herbs, seasoning, stock and rice and mix well. Cook for about 5 minutes, stirring until all the stock has been absorbed.

Cook the cabbage leaves in boiling water for 2 minutes, drain well and trim away the thickest part of the stems. Place a little of the filling in the centre of each cabbage leaf and roll up to form a parcel, tucking in the ends. Place in the slow cooker.

Sieve or purée in a liquidiser the contents of the can of tomatoes, turn into a saucepan and bring to the boil. Season well and pour over the cabbage leaves. Cover the pot and cook on HIGH for 30 minutes, then turn to LOW for a further 3½ hours.

Serves 4–6
Slow cooking time: 4 hours

AMERICAN
Filling:
1 small onion, chopped
1 lb lean ground beef
½ teaspoon mixed dried herbs
1 teaspoon salt
¼ teaspoon pepper
⅔ cup beef stock
⅓ cup cooked rice

12 cabbage leaves
14-oz can tomatoes
salt and pepper

Sweet and Sour Meat Balls
(page 56)

Sweet and Sour Meat Balls

METRIC/IMPERIAL
0.5 kg/1 lb minced beef
75 g/3 oz fresh white
  breadcrumbs
1 egg
salt and pepper
2 tablespoons cooking oil
1 small onion, chopped
2 carrots, peeled and cut in
  strips
1 leek, washed and finely sliced
100 g/4 oz mushrooms, sliced
Sweet and sour sauce:
1½ teaspoons cornflour
2 teaspoons brown sugar
150 ml/¼ pint water
2 tablespoons tomato ketchup
1 tablespoon vinegar
2 teaspoons soya sauce
salt and pepper

Put the beef, breadcrumbs, egg and seasoning in a bowl and mix well. Turn on to a floured surface and shape into twenty meat balls. Heat the oil in a frying pan and fry the meat balls until brown all over. Lift out with a slotted spoon and put in the slow cooker. Add the vegetables to the pan and cook slowly for 5 minutes; add to the pot.

Place the cornflour, sugar and water in a bowl and mix to a smooth paste. Add the remaining sauce ingredients to the bowl and pour into the frying pan. Bring to the boil, stirring until thickened. Pour into the pot, cover and cook on HIGH for 30 minutes, then turn to LOW for a further 4 hours. Serve on a bed of rice with a fresh green salad.

Serves 4–5
Slow cooking time: 4½ hours

AMERICAN
1 lb ground beef
1½ cups fresh white bread
  crumbs
1 egg
salt and pepper
3 tablespoons cooking oil
1 small onion, chopped
2 carrots, peeled and cut in
  strips
1 leek, washed and finely sliced
1 cup sliced mushrooms
Sweet and sour sauce:
1½ teaspoons cornstarch
2 teaspoons brown sugar
⅔ cup water
3 tablespoons tomato ketchup
1 tablespoon vinegar
2 teaspoons soy sauce
salt and pepper

Irish Beef and Dumplings

METRIC/IMPERIAL
0.75 kg/1½ lb stewing steak
25 g/1 oz dripping
2 rashers streaky bacon, rinded
  and cut in strips
225 g/8 oz onions, chopped
225 g/8 oz carrots, diced
1 teaspoon salt
pepper
150 ml/¼ pint Guinness
150 ml/¼ pint beef stock
Dumplings:
100 g/4 oz self-raising flour
50 g/2 oz shredded suet
salt and pepper
4 tablespoons water (approx.)

Cut the stewing steak into large pieces, about 7.5 cm/3 inches square, and remove any excess fat. Melt the dripping in a frying pan and fry the meat with the bacon until brown. Lift out with a slotted spoon and place in the slow cooker. Add the vegetables to the pan with the seasoning, Guinness and stock and bring to the boil.

Pour over the meat, cover the pot and cook on HIGH for 30 minutes, then turn to LOW for a further 5 hours.

Turn the pot to HIGH and prepare the dumplings: mix the flour, suet and seasoning together and add sufficient water to make a firm dough. Divide into eight equal pieces, shape into balls and drop into the pot with the beef. Cover and cook on HIGH for 40 minutes. Taste to check the seasoning and serve at once.

Serves 4
Slow cooking time: 6¼ hours

AMERICAN
1½ lb flank meat
2 tablespoons drippings
2 slices bacon, rinded and cut
  in strips
½ lb onions, chopped
½ lb carrots, diced
1 teaspoon salt
pepper
⅔ cup dark beer or stout
⅔ cup beef stock
Dumplings:
1 cup all-purpose flour sifted
  with 1 teaspoon baking
  powder
⅓ cup chopped suet
salt and pepper
⅓ cup water (approx.)

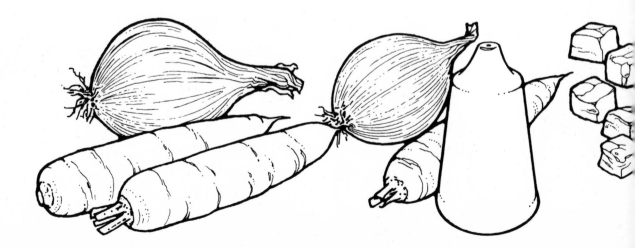

Tasty Beef Curry

Curry is best cooked very slowly to bring out all the flavours, so the slow cooker is ideal for this.

METRIC/IMPERIAL
1 tablespoon cooking oil
0.75 kg/1½ lb thin flank, cut in 2.5-cm/1-inch cubes
1 large onion, finely chopped
1 dessert apple, peeled, cored and chopped
1 tablespoon curry powder
15 g/½ oz plain flour
300 ml/½ pint stock
1 tablespoon tomato purée
1 tablespoon mango chutney
salt and pepper
1 teaspoon lemon juice

AMERICAN
1 tablespoon cooking oil
1½ lb flank steak, cut in 1-inch cubes
1 large onion, finely chopped
1 eating apple, peeled, cored and chopped
1 tablespoon curry powder
2 tablespoons all-purpose flour
1¼ cups stock
1 tablespoon tomato paste
1 tablespoon mango chutney
salt and pepper
1 teaspoon lemon juice

Heat the oil in a frying pan and fry the meat until well browned. Lift out with a slotted spoon and place in the slow cooker. Fry the onion in the pan until just turning brown then add the chopped apple. Mix the curry powder and flour together and add to the pan, stirring for 3–4 minutes. Gradually add the stock and tomato purée with the chutney, seasoning and lemon juice; bring to the boil, stirring until thickened.

Pour over the meat, cover and cook on HIGH for 30 minutes, then turn to LOW and cook for a further 5–6 hours or until tender. Taste to check the seasoning and serve with boiled rice and the usual curry accompaniments.

Serves 4–6
Slow cooking time: 5½–6½ hours

Mild Pineapple Beef Curry

METRIC/IMPERIAL
50 g/2 oz desiccated coconut
300 ml/½ pint boiling water
25 g/1 oz dripping
0.5 kg/1¼ lb stewing steak, cut in 1-cm/½-inch cubes
25 g/1 oz plain flour
1 tablespoon curry powder
227-g/8-oz can pineapple pieces
1 small green pepper, seeded and chopped
2 tablespoons mango chutney
1 tablespoon redcurrant jelly
1 beef stock cube
½ teaspoon salt

AMERICAN
⅔ cup shredded coconut
1¼ cups boiling water
2 tablespoons drippings
1¼ lb flank steak, cut in ½-inch cubes
¼ cup all-purpose flour
1 tablespoon curry powder
8-oz can pineapple chunks
1 small green pepper, seeded and chopped
3 tablespoons mango chutney
1 tablespoon red currant jelly
1 beef bouillon cube
½ teaspoon salt

Put the coconut in a bowl, cover with the water, and leave to stand for 1 hour. Strain and reserve the liquid.

Melt the dripping in a large pan, add the meat and fry until golden brown. Stir in the flour and curry powder and cook gently for about 5 minutes. Add the coconut water and pineapple with the juice from the can. Stir in the remaining ingredients and bring to the boil, stirring until thickened.

Turn into the slow cooker, cover and cook on HIGH for 30 minutes then turn to LOW and cook for a further 5 hours. Taste to check the seasoning and serve with boiled rice.

Serves 4
Slow cooking time: 5½ hours

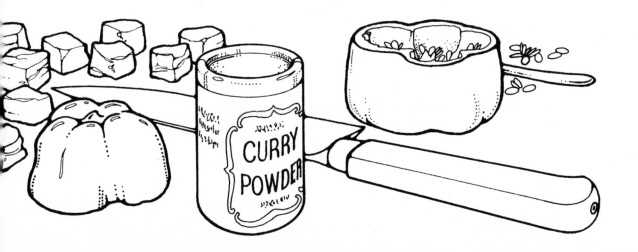

opposite *Mild Pineapple Beef Curry (page 57)*

above *Sherried Beef (page 60)*

Sherried Beef

METRIC/IMPERIAL
0.75 kg/1½ lb stewing steak
3 tablespoons cooking oil
225 g/8 oz onions, sliced
1 clove garlic, crushed
297-g/10½-oz can condensed
   tomato soup
½ teaspoon celery salt
1 tablespoon made mustard
1 teaspoon chopped fresh
   rosemary
4 tablespoons dry sherry
1 teaspoon salt
¼ teaspoon pepper
9–12 stuffed green olives
sprig rosemary to garnish

Cut the steak into six equal pieces. Heat the oil in a frying pan and fry the meat until brown on both sides. Lift out and place in the slow cooker. Add the onions and garlic to the oil remaining in the pan and fry for 3 minutes. Add the soup, celery salt, mustard, rosemary, sherry and seasoning and bring to the boil, stirring. Pour over the meat.

Cover the pot and cook on HIGH for 30 minutes then turn to LOW and cook for a further 5–6 hours. Stir in the olives, taste to check the seasoning and turn into a serving dish. Garnish with a sprig of rosemary.

Serves 6
Slow cooking time: 5½–6½ hours

AMERICAN
1½ lb flank meat
¼ cup cooking oil
½ lb onions, sliced
1 clove garlic, crushed
10½-oz can condensed tomato
   soup
½ teaspoon celery salt
1 tablespoon prepared mustard
1 teaspoon chopped fresh
   rosemary
⅓ cup dry sherry
1 teaspoon salt
¼ teaspoon pepper
9–12 stuffed green olives
sprig rosemary to garnish

West Country Meat Balls

METRIC/IMPERIAL
0.5 kg/1 lb minced beef
0.5 kg/1 lb minced pork
1 teaspoon dried basil
2 eggs
1 teaspoon salt
1 teaspoon pepper
50 g/2 oz dripping
350 g/12 oz onions, chopped
40 g/1½ oz plain flour
450 ml/¾ pint stock
1 teaspoon Worcestershire
   sauce
gravy browning

Mix the minced beef and pork with the basil, eggs and seasoning and on a lightly floured surface form into about thirty-six balls.

Melt dripping in a large frying pan and fry the meat balls, a dozen at a time, until brown all over. Lift out with a slotted spoon and put in the slow cooker. Add the onions to the dripping in the pan and fry over a moderate heat until golden brown. Stir in the flour and cook for 2–3 minutes, until it begins to turn brown. Add the stock and bring to the boil, stirring. Add the Worcestershire sauce and gravy browning and season to taste.

Pour over the meat balls, cover and cook on HIGH for 30 minutes, then turn to LOW and cook for a further 3–4 hours. Taste to check the seasoning. Serve with creamy mashed potatoes and carrots.

Serves 8
Slow cooking time: 3½–4½ hours

AMERICAN
1 lb ground beef
1 lb ground pork
1 teaspoon dried basil
2 eggs
1 teaspoon salt
1 teaspoon pepper
¼ cup drippings
¾ lb onions, chopped
⅓ cup all-purpose flour
2 cups stock
1 teaspoon Worcestershire
   sauce
gravy coloring

Chilli con Carne

If you have a large pot, double or treble this recipe to make enough for a crowd at an informal party.

METRIC/IMPERIAL
1 tablespoon cooking oil
2 onions, chopped
0.5 kg/1 lb minced beef
25 g/1 oz plain flour
1 tablespoon tomato purée
397-g/14-oz can tomatoes
1 teaspoon chilli powder
1 green pepper, seeded and cut
   in strips
salt and pepper
425-g/15-oz can kidney beans

AMERICAN
1 tablespoon cooking oil
2 onions, chopped
1 lb ground beef
$\frac{1}{4}$ cup all-purpose flour
1 tablespoon tomato paste
14-oz can tomatoes
1 teaspoon chili powder
1 green pepper, seeded and cut
   in strips
salt and pepper
15-oz can kidney beans

Heat the oil in a frying pan and fry the onions and meat quickly to brown. Stir in the flour and cook for 2 minutes. Add the tomato purée, tomatoes, chilli powder and green pepper and bring to the boil; season well. Turn into the slow cooker, cover and cook on HIGH for 30 minutes then turn to LOW and cook for a further 3 hours.

Drain the kidney beans and add to the pot, stirring lightly to mix. Cover and cook for a further 1 hour or until the meat is tender. Taste and adjust seasoning; serve with a green salad and plain boiled rice.

Serves 4
Slow cooking time: $4\frac{1}{2}$ hours

Oxford Pudding

METRIC/IMPERIAL
175 g/6 oz streaky bacon
25 g/1 oz fresh white
   breadcrumbs
grated rind and juice of $\frac{1}{2}$ lemon
1 tablespoon chopped parsley
$\frac{1}{2}$ teaspoon dried thyme
350 g/12 oz minced beef
2 teaspoons Worcestershire
   sauce
$\frac{1}{2}$ teaspoon salt
freshly ground black pepper
boiling water

AMERICAN
9 slices bacon
$\frac{1}{2}$ cup fresh white bread crumbs
grated rind and juice of $\frac{1}{2}$ lemon
1 tablespoon chopped parsley
$\frac{1}{2}$ teaspoon dried thyme
$\frac{3}{4}$ lb ground beef
2 teaspoons Worcestershire
   sauce
$\frac{1}{2}$ teaspoon salt
freshly ground black pepper
boiling water

Oil a 900-ml/1$\frac{1}{2}$-pint (US 2-pint) pudding basin. Cut the rinds from the bacon and chop very finely. Place in the prepared basin with all the other ingredients except the water and mix well. Press into the bowl and cover with a piece of greased foil.

Place the basin in the slow cooker on a jam jar lid, pour in sufficient boiling water to come halfway up the sides of the basin, cover and cook on HIGH for 3 hours.

Remove from the pot and leave the meat pudding to cool in the basin, then chill thoroughly. Slip a knife round the edge of the bowl and turn the pudding out on to a plate; cut in slices and serve with a salad.

Serves 4–5
Slow cooking time: 3 hours

Braised Brisket with Vegetables

METRIC/IMPERIAL
1.25 kg/2$\frac{1}{2}$ lb brisket of beef
25 g/1 oz dripping
1 leek, washed and sliced
2 carrots, peeled and sliced
3 sticks celery, sliced
salt and pepper
150 ml/$\frac{1}{4}$ pint boiling stock

AMERICAN
2$\frac{1}{2}$ lb brisket of beef
2 tablespoons drippings
1 leek, washed and sliced
2 carrots, peeled and sliced
3 stalks celery, sliced
salt and pepper
$\frac{2}{3}$ cup boiling stock

Trim the meat to remove any excess fat. Melt the dripping in a frying pan and quickly brown the beef all over. Place the meat in the slow cooker. Add the vegetables to the pan, fry lightly for 5 minutes and spoon round the meat. Season well and pour over the hot stock. Cover and cook on HIGH for 1 hour, then turn to LOW for 8 hours. Serve with boiled new potatoes sprinkled with chopped parsley.

Serves 6
Slow cooking time: 9 hours

Beef Goulash with Dumplings

METRIC/IMPERIAL
25 g/1 oz dripping
0.5 kg/1 lb stewing steak, cubed
1 large onion, sliced
1 large green pepper, seeded and sliced
2 tablespoons paprika
25 g/1 oz plain flour
227-g/8-oz can tomatoes
150 ml/¼ pint beef stock
salt and pepper
Dumplings:
100 g/4 oz self-raising flour
50 g/2 oz shredded suet
2 tablespoons chopped parsley
salt and pepper
4 tablespoons water (approx.)

Melt the dripping in a frying pan and quickly fry the meat. Lift out with a slotted spoon and place in the slow cooker. Add the onion and pepper to the pan and fry for 3–4 minutes, stir in the paprika and flour and cook for 1 minute. Add the tomatoes and stock and bring to the boil. Season and pour into the pot. Cover and cook on HIGH for 30 minutes, then on LOW for 6 hours.

Turn the slow cooker to HIGH. Mix the flour, suet, parsley and seasoning together for the dumplings, and add sufficient water to make a firm dough. Divide the mixture into eight equal pieces, shape into balls and drop into the pot. Cover and cook on HIGH for a final 40 minutes.

Serves 4
Slow cooking time: 7¼ hours

AMERICAN
2 tablespoons drippings
1 lb flank steak, cubed
1 large onion, sliced
1 large green pepper, seeded and sliced
3 tablespoons paprika
¼ cup all-purpose flour
8-oz can tomatoes
⅔ cup beef stock
salt and pepper
Dumplings:
1 cup all-purpose flour sifted with 1 teaspoon baking powder
⅓ cup chopped suet
3 tablespoons chopped parsley
salt and pepper
⅓ cup water (approx.)

Spanish Meat Loaf

METRIC/IMPERIAL
50 g/2 oz stuffed green olives
425-g/15-oz can ratatouille
225 g/8 oz minced beef
225 g/8 oz pork sausagemeat
3 slices white bread soaked in water, then squeezed dry
1 tablespoon chopped parsley
½ teaspoon salt
pepper
boiling water

If you have any leftover slow cooked ratatouille (see page 84), you could substitute it for the canned ratatouille in this recipe.

Distribute the olives evenly over the base of a greased 0.5-kg/1-lb loaf tin and cover with half the can of ratatouille, spreading it evenly.

Mix the beef and sausagemeat together in a bowl. Mash the bread with a fork and add to the meat with the parsley, seasoning and remaining ratatouille. Mix well, put into the loaf tin, smooth the top and cover with a piece of greased foil. Place in the slow cooker and pour in sufficient boiling water to come halfway up the sides of the tin. Cover and cook on HIGH for 30 minutes then turn to LOW for a further 5–6 hours.

Run a knife round the sides of the meat loaf and turn out on to a serving dish. Serve the meat sliced with creamed potatoes or extra ratatouille.

Serves 4–5
Slow cooking time: 5½–6½ hours

AMERICAN
6 tablespoons stuffed green olives
15-oz can ratatouille
½ lb ground beef
1 cup pork sausagemeat
3 slices white bread soaked in water, then squeezed dry
1 tablespoon chopped parsley
½ teaspoon salt
pepper
boiling water

opposite *Spanish Meat Loaf*

Beef Roulades

METRIC/IMPERIAL
4 thin slices topside of beef
salt and pepper
8 rashers streaky bacon
25 g/1 oz dripping
150 ml/¼ pint boiling cider
Stuffing:
75 g/3 oz fresh white
  breadcrumbs
1 onion, finely chopped
¼ teaspoon dried thyme
1 tablespoon chopped parsley
50 g/2 oz streaky bacon, rinded
  and chopped
2 tablespoons milk

Flatten the beef slices on a board with a rolling pin and season on both sides with salt and pepper. Mix together the stuffing ingredients, using the milk to bind, and divide among the beef slices. Roll up each slice of beef firmly and wrap two bacon rashers around each roll; if necessary secure with thin string.

Melt the dripping in a frying pan and fry the beef rolls quickly to brown all over. Lift out and put in the slow cooker. Pour over the cider, cover and cook on HIGH for 30 minutes, then turn to LOW and cook for a further 4 hours. Serve with the cider as a thin gravy.

Serves 4
Slow cooking time: 4½ hours

AMERICAN
4 thin slices top round of beef
salt and pepper
8 slices bacon
2 tablespoons drippings
⅔ cup boiling cider
Stuffing:
1½ cups fresh white bread
  crumbs
1 onion, finely chopped
¼ teaspoon dried thyme
1 tablespoon chopped parsley
3 slices bacon, rinded and
  chopped
3 tablespoons milk

Beef and Bacon Olives

METRIC/IMPERIAL
4 thin slices topside of beef
8 rashers back bacon
freshly ground black pepper
2 tablespoons cooking oil
25 g/1 oz butter
1 large onion, chopped
1 clove garlic, crushed
100 g/4 oz button mushrooms,
  sliced
¼ teaspoon mixed dried herbs
25 g/1 oz plain flour
300 ml/½ pint beef stock
salt

Flatten the beef slices on a board with a rolling pin. Cut the rind from the bacon and place two rashers on each slice of meat. Season well with pepper; roll up and secure each roll with two wooden cocktail sticks. Cut each beef roll in half.

Heat the oil in a pan, add the butter and fry the beef rolls until brown. Lift out and place in the slow cooker. Fry the onion and garlic in the fat left in the pan for 2–3 minutes then add the mushrooms and herbs. Blend in the flour, then add the stock and bring to the boil; simmer for 2 minutes, season and pour over the beef rolls. Cover and cook on HIGH for 30 minutes then turn to LOW for 5 hours.

Serves 4
Slow cooking time: 5½ hours

AMERICAN
4 thin slices top round of beef
8 slices Canadian bacon
freshly ground black pepper
3 tablespoons cooking oil
2 tablespoons butter
1 large onion, chopped
1 clove garlic, crushed
1 cup sliced button mushrooms
¼ teaspoon mixed dried herbs
¼ cup all-purpose flour
1¼ cups beef stock
salt

Braised Tomato Beef

METRIC/IMPERIAL
salt and pepper
1.25 kg/2½ lb silverside or
  topside of beef
25 g/1 oz dripping
3 onions, sliced
397-g/14-oz can tomatoes
1 teaspoon mixed dried herbs
25 g/1 oz cornflour
1 tablespoon water

Season the beef well. Melt the dripping in a frying pan and fry the onions with the beef until golden brown on all sides. Lift out the beef and put in the slow cooker. Add the tomatoes and herbs to the onions in the pan and bring to the boil. Pour over the beef, cover and cook on HIGH for 4–5 hours.

Lift the beef out and place on a serving dish. Keep warm. Blend the cornflour with the water and stir into the pot, cover and cook for 5–10 minutes. Taste to check the seasoning, spoon a little of the sauce over and around the beef and serve the rest separately.

Serves 6
Slow cooking time: 4¼–5¼ hours

AMERICAN
salt and pepper
2½ lb bottom or top round of
  beef
2 tablespoons drippings
3 onions, sliced
14-oz can tomatoes
1 teaspoon mixed dried herbs
¼ cup cornstarch
1 tablespoon water

Boeuf en Daube

METRIC/IMPERIAL
1.25–1.5 kg/2½–3 lb topside
    of beef
1–2 cloves garlic, sliced
1 teaspoon salt
¼ teaspoon black pepper
2 sprigs thyme
50 g/2 oz dripping
1 large onion, sliced
0.5 kg/1 lb small carrots
150 ml/¼ pint red wine
300 ml/½ pint stock
bay leaf

Make small incisions in the beef with a sharp knife and fill them with small slices of garlic. Blend together the salt, pepper and the leaves of one sprig of thyme, and rub into the meat.

Melt the dripping in a frying pan and quickly brown the beef all over, lift out and put to one side. Add the onion and the peeled whole carrots to the pan and fry quickly for 2–3 minutes; lift out with a slotted spoon. Place in the slow cooker and put the beef on top.

Pour off all the fat remaining in the pan and add the wine, stock and bay leaf with the remaining sprig of thyme. Bring to the boil and pour over the meat. Cover and cook on HIGH for 4–5 hours. Remove the bay leaf and sprig of thyme. Taste to check the seasoning. Place the beef on a serving dish and spoon the vegetables and some of the gravy round.

AMERICAN
2½–3 lb top round of beef
1–2 cloves garlic, sliced
1 teaspoon salt
¼ teaspoon black pepper
2 sprigs thyme
¼ cup drippings
1 large onion, sliced
1 lb small carrots
⅔ cup red wine
1¼ cups stock
bay leaf

Serves 8
Slow cooking time: 4–5 hours

Some vegetables, especially root vegetables, take longer to cook in the slow cooker than meat, so it may be helpful to cut them into quite small pieces and to place them underneath the meat or around the sides of the pot where they will be exposed to more direct heat. Browning meat is not necessary if time for preparation is short, although it does give a better colour to the finished dish and helps reduce excess fat. Leftover stews, curries and casseroles are particularly suited to reheating in the slow cooker and may even taste better the second time round, although obviously the cooking time will be shorter than in the original recipe.

OTHER MEATS

Don't be so dazzled by the endless possibilities for beef that you miss the equally impressive range of slow cooked pork, bacon, lamb, veal, kidney and liver dishes. From roasted lamb or veal worthy of an elegant dinner party to delicious, economical sausage or oxtail dishes, the slow cooker makes a success of them all.

Be sure to trim any excess fat from the pork or lamb before placing it in the pot. Skim the sauce before serving if necessary. Flavours are enhanced by slow, gentle cooking, so be careful with seasoning. Ox liver, kidney and tongue all benefit from cooking for long periods, so try them and see how tasty these economical cuts can be. Stock produced in the pot won't boil away, so delicious gravies are no problem. Use your imagination to concoct other exciting dishes your family and friends will enjoy.

Bacon Pot Roast

METRIC/IMPERIAL
1-kg/2-lb piece gammon
8 small onions
2 leeks, washed
2 carrots
1 parsnip
bay leaf
sprigs of rosemary
300 ml/½ pint dry cider
25 g/1 oz brown sugar
1 stock cube
salt and pepper
75 g/3 oz dried apricots

Soak the gammon in water to cover for 1–2 hours. Peel the onions but leave them whole. Discard the green parts of the leeks and slice the white parts. Peel and slice the carrots and parsnip. Place all the vegetables in the slow cooker with the bay leaf and rosemary. Drain the gammon and place in the pot.

Blend the cider, brown sugar and stock cube in a saucepan and bring to the boil, stirring. Turn into the pot. Season lightly and add the dried apricots. Cover and cook on HIGH for 5–6 hours.

Remove the bay leaf and rosemary and taste to check the seasoning. Serve the gammon sliced with creamy mashed potatoes.

AMERICAN
2-lb piece salted or smoked
   bacon
8 small onions
2 leeks, washed
2 carrots
1 parsnip
bay leaf
sprigs of rosemary
1¼ cups dry cider
2 tablespoons brown sugar
1 bouillon cube
salt and pepper
½ cup dried apricots

Serves 4
Slow cooking time: 5–6 hours

Hot Chops

METRIC/IMPERIAL
4 loin pork chops
2 tablespoons cooking oil
1 large onion, sliced
15 g/½ oz cornflour
1 teaspoon dry mustard
300 ml/½ pint water
2 tablespoons tomato purée
1 tablespoon Worcestershire
   sauce
1 tablespoon vinegar
1 tablespoon brown sugar
1 tablespoon lemon juice
salt and pepper

Trim any excess fat from the chops. Heat the oil in a frying pan and quickly fry the chops to brown on both sides. Place in the slow cooker. Add the onion to the pan and fry for 2–3 minutes. Blend the cornflour and mustard with a little of the water in a bowl then add the remaining ingredients with the rest of the water. Pour into the pan and bring to the boil, stirring until thickened.

Pour over the chops, cover and cook on HIGH for 30 minutes, then turn to LOW for a further 3–4 hours. Serve with ribbon noodles and a green vegetable.

AMERICAN
4 loin pork chops
3 tablespoons cooking oil
1 large onion, sliced
1 tablespoon cornstarch
1 teaspoon dry mustard
1¼ cups water
3 tablespoons tomato paste
1 tablespoon Worcestershire
   sauce
1 tablespoon vinegar
1 tablespoon brown sugar
1 tablespoon lemon juice
salt and pepper

Serves 4
Slow cooking time: 3½–4½ hours

Baked Bacon with Apples

METRIC/IMPERIAL
4 (100-g/4-oz) slices collar
   bacon
225 g/8 oz cooking apples,
   peeled, cored and sliced
granulated sugar
¼ teaspoon dried sage
freshly ground black pepper
150 ml/¼ pint boiling water

Soak the bacon slices in water to cover for 2 hours, then remove the rind. Put the sliced apples in the slow cooker and sprinkle with a little sugar, lay the bacon on top and add the sage and black pepper. Pour over the boiling water, cover and cook on HIGH for 2–3 hours.

AMERICAN
4 (¼-lb) slices smoked pork
   shoulder butt
½ lb baking apples, peeled,
   cored and sliced
sugar
¼ teaspoon dried sage
freshly ground black pepper
⅔ cup boiling water

Serves 4
Slow cooking time: 2–3 hours

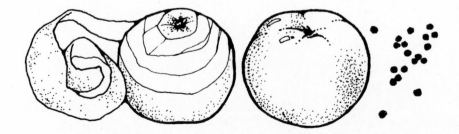

Braised Pork and Cabbage

METRIC/IMPERIAL
0.5 kg/1¼ lb lean boneless pork
40 g/1½ oz butter
2 onions, chopped
0.5 kg/1 lb potatoes, sliced
450 ml/¾ pint stock
salt and pepper
0.5 kg/1 lb cabbage, shredded

This Swiss recipe is delicious and makes a complete meal in itself.

Cut the pork into 2.5-cm/1-inch cubes and trim away any excess fat. Melt the butter in a frying pan and fry the pork for 2–3 minutes; lift out with a slotted spoon and place in the slow cooker. Add the onions to the butter remaining in the pan and fry for 2–3 minutes. Add the potatoes and stock to the pan with plenty of seasoning, bring to the boil and pour over the pork.

Cover the pot and cook on HIGH for 3½ hours. Stir in the shredded cabbage, cover and cook for a further 30–45 minutes until the cabbage is just cooked. Taste to check the seasoning before serving.

Serves 4
Slow cooking time: 4–4¼ hours

AMERICAN
1¼ lb lean boneless pork
3 tablespoons butter
2 onions, chopped
1 lb potatoes, sliced
2 cups stock
salt and pepper
3½ cups shredded cabbage

French Roasted Pork

METRIC/IMPERIAL
1 onion, chopped
3 tablespoons cooking oil
212-g/7½-oz can apricots
25 g/1 oz fresh white
    breadcrumbs
100 g/4 oz pork sausagemeat
salt and pepper
½ teaspoon dried sage
1.25 kg/2½ lb boned spare rib
    of pork, rinded

Put the onion with a third of the oil in a small pan and fry for 2–3 minutes. Drain and chop the apricots, reserving the syrup, and add with the breadcrumbs, sausagemeat, seasoning and sage; mix thoroughly.

Pack the stuffing into the cavity in the pork and secure with skewers or cocktail sticks. Heat the remaining oil in a frying pan and fry the pork quickly to brown all over. Put in the slow cooker, cover and cook on HIGH for 5 hours. Place the pork on a serving dish to keep warm, then skim the fat from the juices in the pot and use with the reserved apricot syrup to make a gravy.

Serves 6
Slow cooking time: 5 hours

AMERICAN
1 onion, chopped
¼ cup cooking oil
7½-oz can apricots
½ cup fresh white bread crumbs
¼ lb pork sausagemeat
salt and pepper
½ teaspoon dried sage
2½ lb boneless pork shoulder
    butt, rinded

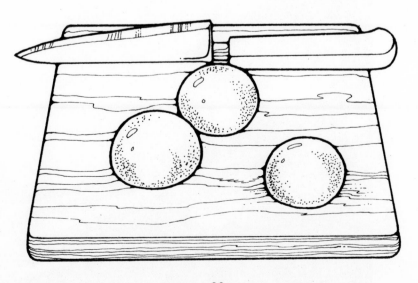

French Roasted Pork (page 69)

Spiced Pork Pilaff

METRIC/IMPERIAL
0.5 kg/1 lb lean boneless pork
100 g/4 oz onions
40 g/1½ oz butter
225 g/8 oz long-grain rice
750 ml/1¼ pints stock
3 tablespoons soya sauce
1 teaspoon curry powder
1 teaspoon salt
225 g/8 oz frozen mixed
  vegetables, thawed

Cut the pork into small cubes and slice the onions in rings. Melt the butter and fry the onions and pork quickly for 5 minutes, then lift out with a slotted spoon and place in the slow cooker. Add the rice to the butter remaining in the pan and fry until the butter is absorbed.

Stir in the stock, soya sauce, curry powder and salt and bring to the boil, stirring. Turn into the pot and mix lightly with the pork and onions. Cover and cook on LOW for 3–4 hours.

Add the vegetables, stirring lightly with a fork, cover and cook on LOW for a further 30 minutes. Taste to check the seasoning and serve with a green salad.

Serves 4–6
Slow cooking time: 3½–4½ hours

AMERICAN
1 lb lean boneless pork
¼ lb onions
3 tablespoons butter
1 cup long-grain rice
3 cups stock
¼ cup soy sauce
1 teaspoon curry powder
1 teaspoon salt
½ lb frozen mixed vegetables,
  thawed

Pork Chops in Cider and Orange Sauce

METRIC/IMPERIAL
4 loin pork chops
25 g/1 oz butter
½ teaspoon made mustard
1½ teaspoons tomato purée
1 teaspoon paprika
150 ml/¼ pint dry cider
juice of 2 oranges
salt and pepper
15 g/½ oz cornflour
1 tablespoon water

Trim the rind and excess fat from the pork chops. Melt the butter in a frying pan and fry the chops until brown on both sides. Lift out and place in the slow cooker. Pour off any fat left in the pan, add the mustard, tomato purée, paprika, cider and orange juice and bring to the boil. Pour over the chops and season well. Cover and cook on HIGH for 30 minutes then turn to LOW for 4 hours.

Blend the cornflour with the water, add a little of the hot sauce, stir back into the pot and leave for 5–10 minutes to thicken. Taste to check the seasoning and serve with creamed potatoes and a green vegetable.

Serves 4
Slow cooking time: 4¾ hours

AMERICAN
4 loin pork chops
2 tablespoons butter
½ teaspoon prepared mustard
1½ teaspoons tomato paste
1 teaspoon paprika
⅔ cup dry cider
juice of 2 oranges
salt and pepper
2 tablespoons cornstarch
1 tablespoon water

Pork with Sage and Apple Sauce

METRIC/IMPERIAL
0.75 kg/1½ lb lean boneless
  pork
25 g/1 oz plain flour
1 teaspoon salt
freshly ground black pepper
1 teaspoon dry mustard
pinch ground ginger
2 tablespoons cooking oil
2 onions, sliced
pinch chopped fresh rosemary
1 teaspoon chopped fresh sage
300 ml/½ pint dry cider
small can apple sauce

Trim any fat from the meat and cut into small 1-cm/½-inch pieces. Mix the flour, seasoning, mustard and ginger together in a paper or polythene bag and toss the pork in it. Heat the oil in a pan and fry the pork with the onions until browned; lift out, place in the slow cooker and sprinkle with the herbs.

Add the cider to the pan and bring to the boil, pour over the meat, cover and cook on HIGH for 30 minutes, then turn to LOW and cook for a further 5–6 hours. Top with apple sauce, and serve with carrots and plain boiled potatoes.

Serves 4–6
Slow cooking time: 5½–6½ hours

AMERICAN
1½ lb lean boneless pork
¼ cup all-purpose flour
1 teaspoon salt
freshly ground black pepper
1 teaspoon dry mustard
pinch ground ginger
3 tablespoons cooking oil
2 onions, sliced
pinch chopped fresh rosemary
1 teaspoon chopped fresh sage
1¼ cups dry cider
small can applesauce

Roast Stuffed Veal

METRIC/IMPERIAL
Stuffing:
15 g/½ oz butter
1 small onion, chopped
100 g/4 oz lamb's liver, finely
   chopped
350 g/12 oz pork sausagemeat
75 g/3 oz fresh white
   breadcrumbs
grated rind of 1 small lemon
1 egg, beaten
1 teaspoon chopped fresh
   thyme
1 tablespoon chopped parsley
1 teaspoon salt
freshly ground black pepper

1.5-kg/3–3½-lb boned
   shoulder or breast of veal
50 g/2 oz butter
2 tablespoons lemon juice
salt and pepper
Gravy:
25 g/1 oz dripping
25 g/1 oz plain flour
5 tablespoons red wine
1 tablespoon redcurrant jelly

First make the stuffing: melt the butter in a small pan, add the onion and liver and fry for 2–3 minutes. Mix the sausagemeat, breadcrumbs, lemon rind and egg in a bowl and blend in the liver and onion. Add the herbs and seasoning and mix well.

Spread the veal out on a board and spread with the stuffing. Roll up and tie firmly with string. Melt the butter in a frying pan and quickly fry the veal to brown all over. Lift out and place in the slow cooker. Pour over any remaining butter, add the lemon juice and season well. Cover and cook on HIGH for 5–6 hours. Lift out, place on a serving dish and keep warm. Pour off the juices from the pot and skim off any fat; this should leave about 300 ml/½ pint (US 1¼ cups) stock.

Make the gravy: melt the dripping in a large pan, blend in the flour and cook gently until a pale golden brown. Remove from the heat and add the meat stock, wine and seasoning; return to the heat and bring to the boil, stirring. Stir in the redcurrant jelly and simmer gently for about 5 minutes. Serve the veal with the gravy handed separately.

Serves 8–10
Slow cooking time: 5–6 hours

AMERICAN
Stuffing:
1 tablespoon butter
1 small onion, chopped
¼ lb lamb's liver, finely chopped
1½ cups pork sausagemeat
1½ cups fresh white bread
   crumbs
grated rind of 1 small lemon
1 egg, beaten
1 teaspoon chopped fresh
   thyme
1 tablespoon chopped parsley
1 teaspoon salt
freshly ground black pepper

3–3½-lb boneless shoulder or
   breast of veal
¼ cup butter
3 tablespoons lemon juice
salt and pepper
Gravy:
2 tablespoons drippings
¼ cup all-purpose flour
6 tablespoons red wine
1 tablespoon red currant jelly

Veal Taranta

METRIC/IMPERIAL
0.75 kg/1½ lb pie veal, cut in
   2-cm/¾-inch cubes
salt and pepper
2 tablespoons cooking oil
1 large onion, sliced
15 g/½ oz plain flour
1 clove garlic, crushed
1 small green pepper, seeded
   and cut in strips
1 small red pepper, seeded and
   cut in strips
397-g/14-oz can tomatoes
chopped parsley and grated
   lemon rind to garnish

Trim any pieces of fat from the veal and season well. Heat the oil in a frying pan and fry the veal lightly to seal, lift out with a slotted spoon and place in the slow cooker. Add the onion to the oil remaining in the pan and fry for 2–3 minutes. Stir in the flour and cook for 1 minute, then add the garlic, peppers and tomatoes.

Bring to the boil, stirring until thickened, and season well. Pour over the veal, cover and cook on HIGH for 30 minutes then on LOW for 5–6 hours. Taste to check the seasoning, turn into a serving dish and sprinkle with the parsley and lemon rind mixed together.

Serves 4–6
Slow cooking time: 5½–6½ hours

AMERICAN
1½ lb boneless veal shank, cut
   in ¾-inch cubes
salt and pepper
3 tablespoons cooking oil
1 large onion, sliced
2 tablespoons all-purpose flour
1 clove garlic, crushed
1 small green pepper, seeded
   and cut in strips
1 small red pepper, seeded and
   cut in strips
14-oz can tomatoes
chopped parsley and grated
   lemon rind to garnish

Spiced Pork Pilaff (page 72)

Braised Oxtail

METRIC/IMPERIAL
1.25 kg/2½ lb oxtail, jointed
40 g/1½ oz dripping
2 onions, chopped
2 large carrots, peeled and
　sliced
½ head celery, sliced
2 rashers streaky bacon
25 g/1 oz plain flour
bay leaf
large sprig parsley
900 ml/1½ pints water
2 beef stock cubes
salt and pepper

Trim off any excess fat from the oxtail, heat the dripping and fry the oxtail until brown. Lift out with a slotted spoon and place in the slow cooker. Add all the vegetables and the bacon, cut in small pieces, to the fat remaining in the pan and fry for 5 minutes. Stir in the flour, cook for 1 minute and add the remaining ingredients, crumbling the stock cubes. Bring to the boil and pour over the oxtail.

Cover and cook on HIGH for 1 hour, then turn to LOW and cook for a further 8 hours, or until the meat can be easily removed from the bone. Lift out the oxtail, place in a serving dish and keep warm.

Turn the sauce into a saucepan and boil rapidly until reduced to about 450 ml/¾ pint (US 2 cups). Taste to check the seasoning and if necessary add a little gravy browning. Pour over the oxtail to serve.

AMERICAN
2½ lb oxtail, jointed
3 tablespoons drippings
2 onions, chopped
2 large carrots, peeled and
　sliced
½ bunch celery, sliced
2 slices bacon
¼ cup all-purpose flour
bay leaf
large sprig parsley
3¾ cups water
2 beef bouillon cubes
salt and pepper

Serves 4–6
Slow cooking time: 9 hours

Sherried Kidney Casserole

METRIC/IMPERIAL
0.75 kg/1½ lb ox kidney
50 g/2 oz butter
2 onions, finely sliced
100 g/4 oz mushrooms, sliced
40 g/1½ oz plain flour
300 ml/½ pint water
1 beef stock cube
2 tablespoons sherry
2 teaspoons tomato purée
salt and pepper
Garnish:
triangles of fried bread
chopped parsley

Remove the core from the kidney and cut into 1-cm/½-inch pieces. Melt the butter in a frying pan and fry the kidney with the onions until pale golden brown. Lift out and place in the slow cooker. Add the mushrooms to the butter remaining in the pan and fry for 1 minute. Lift out and put in the pot with the kidney.

Blend the flour with the butter, cook for 1 minute then stir in the mixed water and stock cube with the sherry, tomato purée and seasoning. Bring to the boil, stirring until thickened, and pour over the kidney. Cover and cook on HIGH for 30 minutes then turn to LOW for 4 hours. Turn into a serving dish, adjusting seasoning if necessary, and garnish with triangles of fried bread and chopped parsley.

AMERICAN
1½ lb beef kidney
¼ cup butter
2 onions, finely sliced
1 cup mushrooms, sliced
⅓ cup all-purpose flour
1¼ cups water
1 beef bouillon cube
3 tablespoons sherry
2 teaspoons tomato paste
salt and pepper
Garnish:
triangles of fried bread
chopped parsley

Serves 4–6
Slow cooking time: 4½ hours

Home-Cooked Ox Tongue

METRIC/IMPERIAL
1.5-kg/3½-lb ox tongue, salted
    or pickled
1 onion, quartered
1 carrot, peeled and sliced
bay leaf
300 ml/½ pint boiling water

Order the tongue well in advance (give your butcher at least 10 days' notice) as this will give him time to brine it for you.

Wash the tongue and place in the slow cooker with the remaining ingredients. Cover and cook on HIGH for 6–7 hours. When done the tongue will feel tender when a skewer is pushed into the tip and the bones in the roots will easily pull out.

Lift out, remove any small bones and skin the tongue. Curl the tongue round and fit it tightly into a 15-cm/6-inch round cake tin; cover with a saucer and a heavy weight. Usually sufficient jelly will set round the tongue so that no extra jelly is needed. However, if preferred, the cooking liquid from the pot may be strained into a saucepan, boiled rapidly for 3–4 minutes to reduce it and then spooned over the tongue.

Leave to set and become quite cold. Turn out on to a dish and serve garnished with salad.

AMERICAN
3½-lb beef tongue, salted or
    pickled
1 onion, quartered
1 carrot, peeled and sliced
bay leaf
1¼ cups boiling water

Serves 6–8
Slow cooking time: 6–7 hours

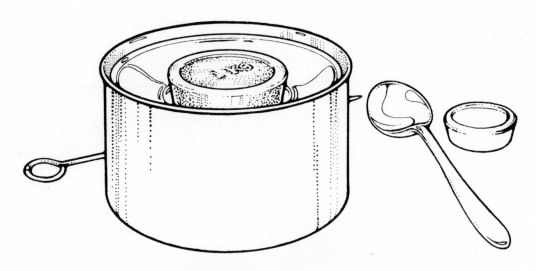

Braised Liver

METRIC/IMPERIAL
0.5 kg/1 lb young ox or pig's
    liver
milk
25 g/1 oz bacon fat or dripping
2 onions, sliced
25 g/1 oz plain flour
397-g/14-oz can tomatoes
salt and pepper
1 tablespoon Worcestershire
    sauce
1 teaspoon sugar
1 teaspoon mixed dried herbs

Ox liver needs long, gentle cooking so the slow cooker is ideal.

Place the liver in a dish, cover with milk and leave to soak for 2 hours; drain well. Melt the bacon fat in a frying pan and fry the liver lightly to seal. Lift out and place in the slow cooker. Add the onions to the fat remaining in the pan and fry until golden brown. Stir in the flour and cook for 1 minute. Add the tomatoes, seasoning, Worcestershire sauce, sugar and herbs and bring to the boil. Pour over the liver, cover and cook on LOW for 5–6 hours.

AMERICAN
1 lb young beef or pork liver
milk
2 tablespoons bacon fat or
    drippings
2 onions, sliced
¼ cup all-purpose flour
14-oz can tomatoes
salt and pepper
1 tablespoon Worcestershire
    sauce
1 teaspoon sugar
1 teaspoon mixed dried herbs

Serves 4
Slow cooking time: 5–6 hours

Rosemary Lamb

A simply delicious way of cooking lamb for entertaining.

METRIC/IMPERIAL
½ leg of lamb (1.25–1.5
   kg/2½–3 lb)
25 g/1 oz dripping
0.75 kg/1½ lb potatoes, sliced
225 g/8 oz onions, sliced
1 large clove garlic, crushed
sprigs rosemary
salt and pepper

AMERICAN
½ leg of lamb (2½–3 lb)
2 tablespoons drippings
1½ lb potatoes, sliced
½ lb onions, sliced
1 large clove garlic, crushed
sprigs rosemary
salt and pepper

Wipe the meat and trim off the knuckle and any excess fat. Melt the dripping in a frying pan and fry the lamb on all sides until golden brown. Remove and put on one side. Add the potatoes and onions to the pan and fry quickly for 3–4 minutes. Put in the base of the slow cooker.

Spread the lamb with the crushed garlic and place on top of the vegetables, cover with sprigs of rosemary and season well. Cover and cook on HIGH for 5 hours. Place the joint on a serving dish and spoon the vegetables round, or serve straight from the pot.

Serves 6
Slow cooking time: 5 hours

Lamb and Apricot Casserole

METRIC/IMPERIAL
0.75–1 kg/1½–2 lb lean boned
   lamb shoulder
2 onions, sliced
2 teaspoons paprika
25 g/1 oz flour
425-g/15-oz can apricots
1 teaspoon salt
pepper
1 tablespoon wine vinegar

AMERICAN
1½–2 lb lean boneless shoulder
   lamb
2 onions, sliced
2 teaspoons paprika
¼ cup all-purpose flour
15-oz can apricots
1 teaspoon salt
pepper
1 tablespoon wine vinegar

Cut the lamb into 2.5-cm/1-inch cubes, place in a frying pan fat side down and cook over a moderate heat for about 5 minutes until the fat runs out; turn and fry on the other side to brown. Lift out with a slotted spoon and place in the slow cooker. Add the onions and paprika to the pan and fry for 2–3 minutes, then blend in the flour and cook for 1 minute.

Drain the apricots and make the juice up to 300 ml/½ pint (US 1¼ cups) with water. Add the liquid to the pan and bring to the boil, stirring. Add the salt, pepper and vinegar and pour the sauce over the lamb. Cover the pot and cook on HIGH for 30 minutes then turn to LOW and cook for a further 4–5 hours or until the lamb is tender. Stir in the apricots and heat through for 15 minutes. Taste to check the seasoning and serve with pasta shells tossed in soured cream.

Serves 4–6
Slow cooking time: 4¾–5¾ hours

opposite *Rosemary Lamb*

Lamb Hot Pot

Serve straight from the slow cooker – no extra vegetables to do at the last moment.

METRIC/IMPERIAL
1 tablespoon cooking oil
4 lamb chump end chops
15 g/½ oz plain flour
150 ml/¼ pint stock
397-g/14-oz can tomatoes
1 clove garlic, crushed
2 teaspoons tomato purée
4 sticks celery, sliced
1 teaspoon salt
freshly ground black pepper
chopped parsley to garnish

Heat the oil in a frying pan. Coat the chops with flour and quickly fry until golden brown. Place in the slow cooker. Add remaining ingredients to pan and bring to the boil.

Pour over the lamb, cover and cook on HIGH for 30 minutes, then on LOW for 6–7 hours. Taste to check the seasoning and sprinkle with plenty of parsley.

Serves 4
Slow cooking time: 6½–7½ hours

AMERICAN
1 tablespoon cooking oil
4 loin lamb chops
2 tablespoons all-purpose flour
⅔ cup stock
14-oz can tomatoes
1 clove garlic, crushed
2 teaspoons tomato paste
4 stalks celery, sliced
1 teaspoon salt
freshly ground black pepper
chopped parsley to garnish

Slow Roasted Lamb

METRIC/IMPERIAL
2 lean breasts of lamb
50 g/2 oz lamb's liver, finely chopped
1 small onion, finely chopped
25 g/1 oz butter
grated rind of 1 lemon
225 g/8 oz pork sausagemeat
50 g/2 oz fresh white breadcrumbs
1 tablespoon chopped parsley
½ teaspoon salt
freshly ground black pepper
dripping

Trim any excess fat from the lamb, remove any small bones and lay the breasts out flat.

Cook the liver and the onion in the butter for 2–3 minutes, add all the remaining ingredients except the dripping and mix well. Divide the stuffing between the breasts and spread over each. Roll up and secure with string.

Melt a very little dripping in a frying pan and fry the lamb quickly to brown. Remove from the pan and place in the slow cooker. Cover and cook on HIGH for 4 hours. Lift out, place on a serving dish and serve with gravy.

Serves 6
Slow cooking time: 4 hours

AMERICAN
2 lean pieces breast of lamb
2 oz lamb's liver, finely chopped
1 small onion, finely chopped
2 tablespoons butter
grated rind of 1 lemon
1 cup pork sausagemeat
1 cup fresh white bread crumbs
1 tablespoon chopped parsley
½ teaspoon salt
freshly ground black pepper
drippings

Fricassée of Lamb

METRIC/IMPERIAL
0.75 kg/1½ lb lean lamb, cut in 2.5-cm/1-inch cubes
15 g/½ oz seasoned plain flour
25 g/1 oz butter
1 large onion, chopped
1 clove garlic, crushed
300 ml/½ pint water
sprig parsley
2 sticks celery, sliced
grated rind and juice of 1 lemon
Caper sauce:
25 g/1 oz butter
25 g/1 oz plain flour
150 ml/¼ pint milk
1 tablespoon chopped parsley
2 teaspoons capers
1 teaspoon made mustard
½ teaspoon salt
pinch pepper

Toss the lamb in the seasoned flour, melt the butter in a frying pan, and add the lamb. Fry quickly until brown, lift out with a slotted spoon and place in the slow cooker. Add the onion and garlic to the pan and fry slowly until soft, about 5 minutes. Add the water, parsley, celery and lemon rind and juice and bring to the boil.

Pour over the lamb, cover and cook on HIGH for 30 minutes and then on LOW for a further 4–5 hours. Lift out the lamb, onion and celery with a slotted spoon and place in a warm serving dish. Strain the liquor from the pot.

Make the caper sauce: melt the butter in a small saucepan, add the flour and cook for 2 minutes. Stir in the milk and the strained cooking liquor and bring to the boil, stirring; simmer for 2 minutes. Add the remaining ingredients and bring to the boil again. Taste to check the seasoning and pour over the lamb.

Serves 4
Slow cooking time: 4½–5½ hours

AMERICAN
1½ lb lean lamb, cut in 1-inch cubes
2 tablespoons seasoned all-purpose flour
2 tablespoons butter
1 large onion, chopped
1 clove garlic, crushed
1¼ cups water
sprig parsley
2 stalks celery, sliced
grated rind and juice of 1 lemon
Caper sauce:
2 tablespoons butter
¼ cup all-purpose flour
⅔ cup milk
1 tablespoon chopped parsley
2 teaspoons capers
1 teaspoon prepared mustard
½ teaspoon salt
pinch pepper

Sausage and Vegetable Casserole

METRIC/IMPERIAL
350 g/12 oz onions, sliced
boiling water
50 g/2 oz butter
50 g/2 oz plain flour
0.5 kg/1 lb potatoes, sliced
salt and pepper
8 frankfurters

This is an ideal lunch dish for the family – put it on first thing in the morning, then go out and come home to a hot meal. The frankfurters may be added whilst laying the table.

Put the onions in a pan, cover with boiling water, bring to the boil and simmer for 2 minutes. Drain well and reserve 450 ml/¾ pint (US 1 pint) of the cooking liquor.

Melt the butter in a saucepan, stir in the flour and cook for 2 minutes. Add the onion liquor and bring to the boil, stirring. Add the potatoes, onions and plenty of seasoning to the pan and return to the boil. Turn into the slow cooker, cover and cook on HIGH for 3½ hours. Add the frankfurters, cover and cook for a further 30 minutes. Taste to check the seasoning before serving.

Serves 4
Slow cooking time: 4 hours

AMERICAN
¾ lb onions, sliced
boiling water
¼ cup butter
½ cup all-purpose flour
1 lb potatoes, sliced
salt and pepper
8 frankfurters

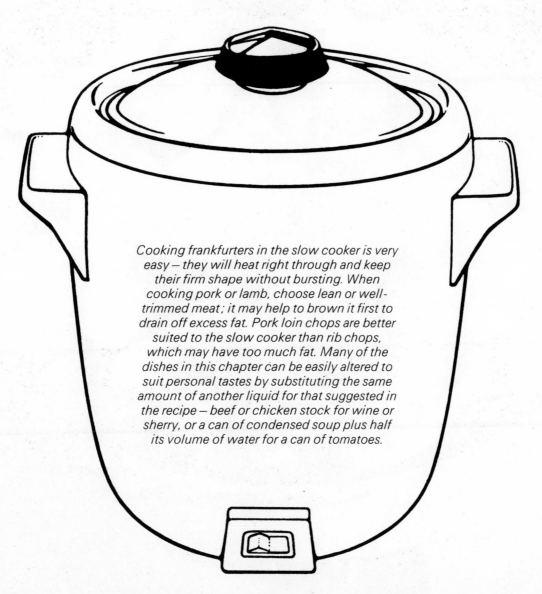

Cooking frankfurters in the slow cooker is very easy – they will heat right through and keep their firm shape without bursting. When cooking pork or lamb, choose lean or well-trimmed meat; it may help to brown it first to drain off excess fat. Pork loin chops are better suited to the slow cooker than rib chops, which may have too much fat. Many of the dishes in this chapter can be easily altered to suit personal tastes by substituting the same amount of another liquid for that suggested in the recipe – beef or chicken stock for wine or sherry, or a can of condensed soup plus half its volume of water for a can of tomatoes.

opposite *Ratatouille* (*page 84*)

VEGETABLES

Vegetables are particularly suitable for one pot cooking as they retain their shape and never form an unappetising mush. Many vegetables cooked by this method take longer than meat, so it is usually best to cut them into very thin (3–5-mm/$\frac{1}{8}$–$\frac{1}{4}$-inch) slices and to place them near the base of the pot when in combination with other foods. Frozen vegetables such as sweetcorn or peas should be added for the last 30 minutes of the cooking time so that they retain their colour and texture. To ensure that the working temperature is not reduced too far, these should be at least partially thawed before being added.

Whole vegetables can also benefit from slow cooking in various tasty casseroles. Even potatoes can be cooked whole in the slow cooker. Most of the recipes call for a certain amount of liquid. A few, however, demonstrate how easy it is to produce a delicious dish without any liquid at all, without fear of burning or sticking. Try them as a main midday meal on their own or as a complement to a meat dish.

Ratatouille

METRIC/IMPERIAL
2 small aubergines
2 courgettes
salt
6 tablespoons cooking oil
2 onions, sliced
2 small green peppers
2 cloves garlic, crushed
freshly ground black pepper
225 g/8 oz tomatoes

Cut the aubergines and courgettes into slices, put on a plate and sprinkle with salt; leave to stand for 30 minutes, drain well and dry on kitchen paper.

Heat the oil in a large pan and fry the onions slowly until soft but not brown. Add the aubergines and courgettes. Remove the seeds and white pith from the green peppers, slice them thinly and add to the pan with the garlic. Heat through and turn into the slow cooker. Season well, cover and cook on HIGH for 30 minutes then turn to LOW for 6 hours.

Peel, quarter and remove the seeds from the tomatoes; add to the pot and continue cooking for a further 2 hours. Stir lightly and taste to check the seasoning before serving.

AMERICAN
2 small eggplant
2 zucchini
salt
½ cup cooking oil
2 onions, sliced
2 small green peppers
2 cloves garlic, crushed
freshly ground black pepper
½ lb tomatoes

Serves 6
Slow cooking time: 8½ hours

Marrow and Tomato Casserole

METRIC/IMPERIAL
1 small marrow
4 tomatoes
1 small onion
50 g/2 oz butter
salt
freshly ground black pepper

Peel the marrow, cut it in half and remove all the seeds; cut in 2.5-cm/1-inch cubes. Skin and slice the tomatoes and very finely chop the onion. Well butter the slow cooker with half the butter then add the vegetables and toss them lightly together; season with salt and plenty of freshly ground black pepper. Dot with the remaining butter, cover and cook on LOW for 7–8 hours. Serve with chops, sausages or grilled chicken pieces.

AMERICAN
1 small summer squash
4 tomatoes
1 small onion
¼ cup butter
salt
freshly ground black pepper

Serves 4–6
Slow cooking time: 7–8 hours

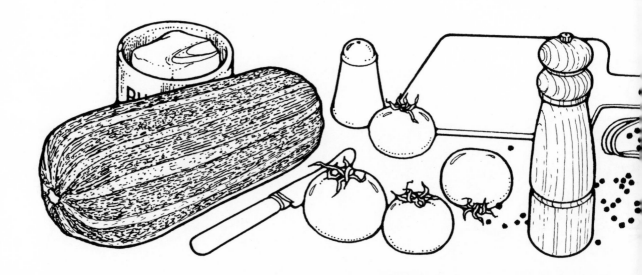

Braised Celery

METRIC/IMPERIAL
2 heads celery
100 g/4 oz carrots, peeled and
 sliced
450 ml/¾ pint stock
salt and pepper
chopped parsley to garnish

Thoroughly wash the celery and cut the stalks into 2.5-cm/1-inch pieces. Place in a saucepan with the carrots, stock and seasoning and bring to the boil. Turn into the slow cooker, cover and cook on HIGH for 1 hour, then turn to LOW and cook for a further 8–9 hours. Turn into a serving dish and sprinkle with chopped parsley.

AMERICAN
2 bunches celery
¼ lb carrots, peeled and sliced
2 cups stock
salt and pepper
chopped parsley to garnish

Serves 6
Slow cooking time: 9–10 hours

Vichy Carrots

METRIC/IMPERIAL
0.5 kg/1 lb carrots
300 ml/½ pint boiling water
25 g/1 oz butter
1½ teaspoons castor sugar
salt and pepper

Peel and thinly slice the carrots. Put them in the slow cooker and add the water, butter, sugar and seasoning. Cover and cook on HIGH for 4 hours. Drain before serving, topped with a knob of butter.

AMERICAN
1 lb carrots
1¼ cups boiling water
2 tablespoons butter
1½ teaspoons sugar
salt and pepper

Serves 4
Slow cooking time: 4 hours

Green Vegetable Ragoût

METRIC/IMPERIAL
40 g/1½ oz butter
1 large onion, sliced
1 cucumber, sliced
350 g/12 oz courgettes, sliced
1 green pepper, seeded and cut
 in strips
6 tablespoons cider
salt and pepper

This ragoût goes well with roast lamb or pork.

Melt the butter in a frying pan, add the onion and fry for 2–3 minutes until soft; add the remaining vegetables and fry for about 5 minutes without browning. Stir in the cider and season well.

    Turn into the slow cooker, cover and cook on LOW for 7–8 hours. Taste to check the seasoning before serving.

AMERICAN
3 tablespoons butter
1 large onion, sliced
1 cucumber, sliced
¾ lb zucchini, sliced
1 green pepper, seeded and cut
 in strips
½ cup cider
salt and pepper

Serves 6–8
Slow cooking time: 7–8 hours

Red Cabbage

METRIC/IMPERIAL
1 small red cabbage
350 g/12 oz cooking apples
150 ml/¼ pint water
40 g/1½ oz sugar
4 whole cloves
1 teaspoon salt
6 tablespoons cider or wine
  vinegar
50 g/2 oz butter
1 tablespoon redcurrant jelly

It is well worth cooking a full pot of red cabbage as what is not eaten can be reheated in a non-stick pan or stored in the freezer.

Trim the cabbage and shred finely. Peel, core and slice the apples; put them in a saucepan with the cabbage, water, sugar, cloves, salt and vinegar and bring to the boil. Turn into the slow cooker, cover and cook on LOW for 8–10 hours. Remove the cloves and stir in the butter and redcurrant jelly before serving with pork or any cold meats and cranberry sauce.

AMERICAN
1 small red cabbage
¾ lb baking apples
⅔ cup water
3 tablespoons sugar
4 whole cloves
1 teaspoon salt
½ cup cider or wine vinegar
¼ cup butter
1 tablespoon red currant jelly

Serves 8
Slow cooking time: 8–10 hours

Stuffed Green Peppers

METRIC/IMPERIAL
2 onions, chopped
0.5 kg/1 lb minced beef
50 g/2 oz plain flour
300 ml/½ pint beef stock
2 carrots, peeled and coarsely
  grated
salt and pepper
3 large green peppers
Cheese sauce:
25 g/1 oz butter
40 g/1½ oz plain flour
300 ml/½ pint milk
½ teaspoon made mustard
salt and pepper
50 g/2 oz cheese, grated

Fry the onions and beef together in a greased pan for 5 minutes, stirring frequently. Stir in the flour and cook for 1 minute, add the stock and bring to the boil. Stir in the carrots, season well and leave to simmer gently whilst preparing the rest of the recipe. Cut the peppers in half, remove the seeds and blanch in boiling water for 2 minutes. Drain well and set aside.

Prepare the cheese sauce: melt the butter in a small pan, blend in the flour and cook for 2 minutes. Remove the pan from the heat and slowly stir in the milk; return to the heat and bring to the boil, stirring. Allow to thicken then add the mustard, seasoning and cheese. Pour the sauce into the slow cooker.

Fill the peppers with the meat mixture and stand them in the cheese sauce in the pot. Cover and cook on LOW for 6 hours. Serve with chunks of French bread.

AMERICAN
2 onions, chopped
1 lb ground beef
½ cup all-purpose flour
1¼ cups beef stock
2 carrots, peeled and coarsely
  grated
salt and pepper
3 large green peppers
Cheese sauce:
2 tablespoons butter
6 tablespoons all-purpose flour
1¼ cups milk
½ teaspoon prepared mustard
salt and pepper
½ cup grated cheese

Serves 6
Slow cooking time: 6 hours

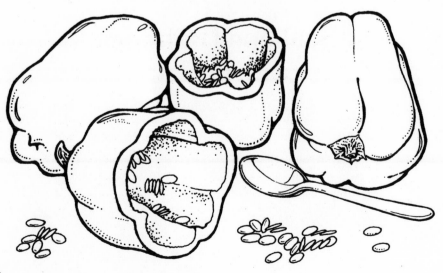

opposite *Red Cabbage*

One Pot Potatoes

METRIC/IMPERIAL
4 medium potatoes
cooking oil

Scrub the potatoes (use as many as are required or will fit in your slow cooker in a single layer, allowing room for a little movement). Make a slit in the skin of each potato and oil them all well.

Arrange the potatoes in the pot, cover and cook on HIGH for 3½–4 hours (the time will vary slightly with the size of the potatoes and make of the cooker). Place in a serving dish and dot with butter. Serve with roasts or cold meats.

AMERICAN
4 medium potatoes
cooking oil

Serves 4
Slow cooking time: 3½–4 hours

Garlic Potatoes

METRIC/IMPERIAL
0.75 kg/1½ lb large potatoes
50 g/2 oz butter
1 clove garlic, crushed
salt and pepper
chopped parsley to garnish

These potatoes are very good served with simple chop or chicken dishes.

Peel the potatoes and cut in large dice. Place in a saucepan, cover with cold water and bring to the boil; drain.

Well butter the slow cooker and place the potatoes and garlic in it; season well, cover and cook on HIGH for about 2 hours. Shake the pot occasionally during cooking so that the potatoes are turned evenly in the garlic butter. Turn into a warm serving dish and sprinkle with chopped parsley.

AMERICAN
1½ lb large potatoes
¼ cup butter
1 clove garlic, crushed
salt and pepper
chopped parsley to garnish

Serves 4
Slow cooking time: 2 hours

Scalloped Potatoes with Leeks

METRIC/IMPERIAL
40 g/1½ oz butter
0.5 kg/1 lb potatoes, thinly
    sliced
225 g/8 oz leeks, washed and
    thinly sliced
salt and pepper
150 ml/¼ pint milk

Grease the slow cooker with a little of the butter and melt the remainder in a large frying pan. Add the potatoes and leeks and fry gently for 5 minutes. Turn into the pot and season (take care: too much salt may cause the milk to curdle).

Pour the milk into the frying pan, bring to the boil and pour over the vegetables. Cover and cook on HIGH for 4 hours. Taste to check the seasoning before serving with meat or fish dishes.

AMERICAN
3 tablespoons butter
1 lb potatoes, thinly sliced
½ lb leeks, washed and thinly
    sliced
salt and pepper
⅔ cup milk

Serves 4–5
Slow cooking time: 4 hours

Potato and Bacon Boulangère

METRIC/IMPERIAL
25 g/1 oz butter
2 onions, thinly sliced
100 g/4 oz streaky bacon, rinded and chopped
0.75 kg/1½ lb potatoes, thinly sliced
salt and pepper
150 ml/¼ pint boiling stock

This is a very good way of cooking potatoes for a large dinner party, as they can be kept hot for up to 2 hours.

Grease the slow cooker with a little of the butter and melt the remainder in a saucepan. Add the onions and bacon and fry for 5 minutes. Layer the potatoes alternately with the onion and bacon mixture in the pot, adding a little seasoning. Pour over the boiling stock, cover and cook on HIGH for 4 hours.

Serves 5–6
Slow cooking time: 4 hours

AMERICAN
2 tablespoons butter
2 onions, thinly sliced
6 slices bacon, rinded and chopped
1½ lb potatoes, thinly sliced
salt and pepper
⅔ cup boiling stock

Buttered New Potatoes

METRIC/IMPERIAL
0.75 kg/1½ lb small new potatoes
50 g/2 oz butter
salt
sprig mint
finely snipped chives to garnish

This is a lovely way to cook new potatoes – the long slow cooking brings out their flavour.

Scrape the potatoes, place them in a saucepan of cold water and bring to the boil; drain well.
     Well butter the slow cooker. Add the potatoes, sprinkle with salt, and add the sprig of mint. Cover and cook on HIGH for 2 hours, shaking the pot occasionally during cooking so that the potatoes are turned evenly in the butter. Turn into a warm serving dish and sprinkle with chives.

Serves 4–6
Slow cooking time: 2 hours

AMERICAN
1½ lb small new potatoes
¼ cup butter
salt
sprig mint
finely snipped chives to garnish

One Pot Potatoes, Buttered New
Potatoes, Scalloped Potatoes
with Leeks, Potato and Bacon
Boulangère in pot (pages 88–9)

Baked Aubergines with Tomatoes

METRIC/IMPERIAL
350 g/12 oz aubergines
225 g/8 oz tomatoes
50 g/2 oz butter (approx.)
salt
freshly ground black pepper
chopped parsley to garnish

This is a very good way of using up soft tomatoes.

Slice the aubergines and cook in boiling salted water for 5 minutes; drain well. Peel and slice the tomatoes. Well butter the slow cooker with half the butter and put in the aubergine and tomato slices; season well and dot with the remaining butter. Cover and cook on LOW for 3–4 hours. Sprinkle with parsley and serve with chops, gammon steaks or sausages.

AMERICAN
¾ lb eggplant
½ lb tomatoes
¼ cup butter (approx.)
salt
freshly ground black pepper
chopped parsley to garnish

Serves 4–6
Slow cooking time: 3–4 hours

Baked Whole Onions

METRIC/IMPERIAL
50 g/2 oz butter
6 small onions
salt and freshly ground black
  pepper

Thoroughly butter the slow cooker. Peel the onions carefully, leaving them whole, and put in the pot. Season well, cover and cook on HIGH for 3–4 hours. Shake the pot occasionally during cooking so that the onions become golden brown all over.

AMERICAN
¼ cup butter
6 small onions
salt and freshly ground black
  pepper

Serves 6
Slow cooking time: 3–4 hours

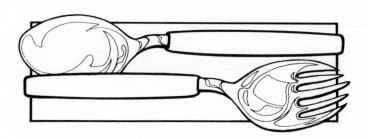

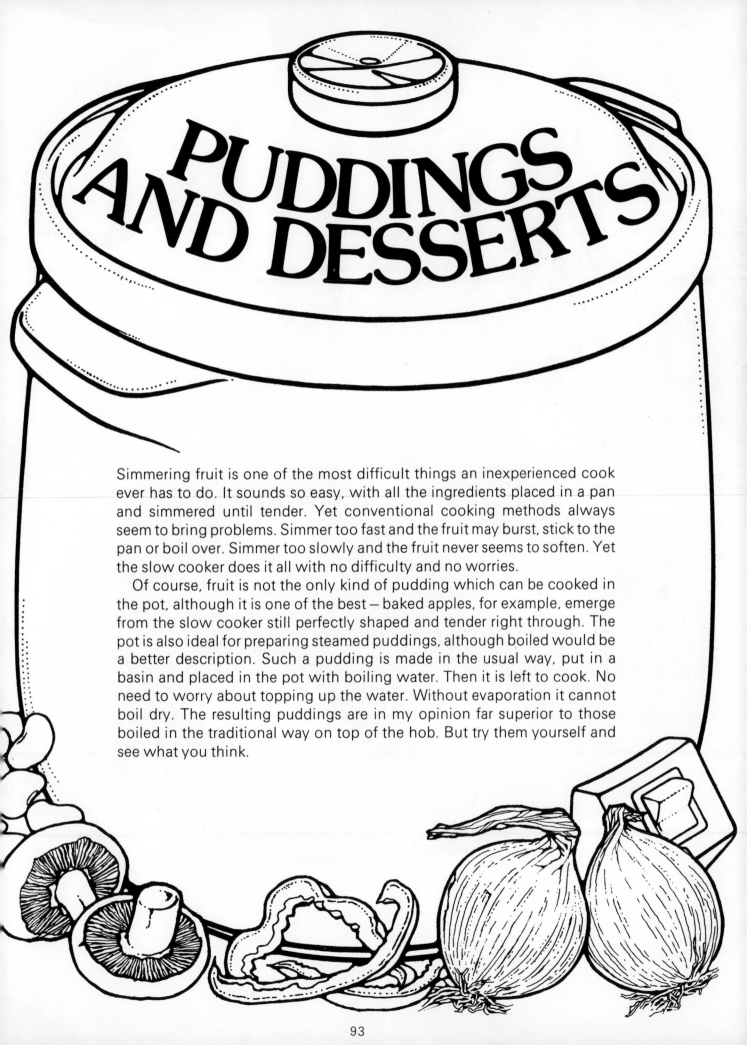

PUDDINGS AND DESSERTS

Simmering fruit is one of the most difficult things an inexperienced cook ever has to do. It sounds so easy, with all the ingredients placed in a pan and simmered until tender. Yet conventional cooking methods always seem to bring problems. Simmer too fast and the fruit may burst, stick to the pan or boil over. Simmer too slowly and the fruit never seems to soften. Yet the slow cooker does it all with no difficulty and no worries.

Of course, fruit is not the only kind of pudding which can be cooked in the pot, although it is one of the best — baked apples, for example, emerge from the slow cooker still perfectly shaped and tender right through. The pot is also ideal for preparing steamed puddings, although boiled would be a better description. Such a pudding is made in the usual way, put in a basin and placed in the pot with boiling water. Then it is left to cook. No need to worry about topping up the water. Without evaporation it cannot boil dry. The resulting puddings are in my opinion far superior to those boiled in the traditional way on top of the hob. But try them yourself and see what you think.

Pears in Red Wine

METRIC/IMPERIAL
150 ml/¼ pint red wine
50 g/2 oz castor sugar
4 pears
pinch ground cinnamon

This is a delicious way of cooking pears. The recipe is easy to adapt for more pears if they will fit lying flat in the slow cooker.

Put the wine and sugar in a small saucepan and bring slowly to the boil to dissolve the sugar.

Peel the pears, keeping them whole and leaving the stems intact. Place the pears to lie as flat as possible in the slow cooker base. Add the cinnamon to the sugar syrup and pour over the pears. Cover and cook on LOW for 5–6 hours (the time will vary with the variety and size of pears used).

Carefully lift out the pears and arrange in a serving dish. Spoon over the red wine and leave to cool. Chill well and serve with lots of thick whipped cream.

AMERICAN
⅔ cup red wine
¼ cup sugar
4 pears
pinch ground cinnamon

Serves 4
Slow cooking time: 5–6 hours

Zabaglione

METRIC/IMPERIAL
4 egg yolks
25 g/1 oz castor sugar
boiling water
150 ml/¼ pint sherry

Put the egg yolks and sugar in a basin and stand it in the slow cooker. Turn to HIGH and pour in sufficient boiling water to come halfway up the sides of the basin. Whisk the mixture steadily until it begins to thicken. Add the sherry gradually and continue whisking until the mixture is the consistency of whipped cream. This should take 5–10 minutes.

Pour the zabaglione into four individual glasses and serve at once with sponge finger biscuits.

AMERICAN
4 egg yolks
2 tablespoons sugar
boiling water
⅔ cup sherry

opposite *Pears in Red Wine*

Serves 4
Slow cooking time: 10–15 minutes

Apple Pudding

METRIC/IMPERIAL
175 g/6 oz self-raising flour
75 g/3 oz shredded suet
6 tablespoons cold water
 (approx.)
0.75 kg/1½ lb cooking apples
75–100 g/3–4 oz castor sugar
whole cloves
boiling water

Grease a 900-ml/1½-pint (US 2-pint) pudding basin. Put the flour and suet in a bowl and mix with sufficient water to make a soft but not sticky dough. Knead lightly on a floured surface, then cut off a third of the pastry and roll out to the size of the top of the basin.

Roll out the remaining pastry and use it to line the basin. Peel, core and slice the apples and put in the basin with the sugar and a few cloves. Damp the edges of the pastry lid and cover the fruit, sealing firmly. Cover with a piece of greased greaseproof paper and a lid of pleated foil.

Place the basin in the slow cooker on a jam jar lid and pour in enough boiling water to come halfway up the sides of the basin. Cover and cook on HIGH for 3½–4 hours. Run a knife round the sides of the pudding, turn out on to a dish and serve with custard.

AMERICAN
1½ cups all-purpose flour sifted
 with 1½ teaspoons baking
 powder
½ cup chopped suet
½ cup cold water (approx.)
1½ lb baking apples
scant ½ cup sugar
whole cloves
boiling water

Serves 4–6
Slow cooking time : 3½–4 hours

Marmalade Upside Down Pudding

METRIC/IMPERIAL
1 large cooking apple
2 tablespoons orange
 marmalade
75 g/3 oz butter
grated rind of 1 orange
75 g/3 oz castor sugar
1 large egg, beaten
150 g/5 oz self-raising flour
2 tablespoons water
boiling water

This pudding goes well with lightly whipped cream or custard.

Butter and lightly flour a 15-cm/6-inch round cake tin. Peel, quarter, core and slice the apple and arrange in the base of the tin. Spread over the marmalade. Cream the butter, orange rind and sugar until light and fluffy. Beat in the egg, a little at a time, and fold in the flour and water. Turn the mixture into the tin, smooth the top and cover with a piece of greased greaseproof paper and a lid of pleated foil.

Stand the tin in the slow cooker on a jam jar lid and pour boiling water round the sides to come halfway up the tin. Cover and cook on HIGH for 4 hours. Ease round the sides of the tin with a knife and turn out on to a warm serving dish.

AMERICAN
1 large baking apple
3 tablespoons orange
 marmalade
⅓ cup butter
grated rind of 1 orange
6 tablespoons sugar
1 large egg, beaten
1¼ cups all-purpose flour sifted
 with 1 teaspoon baking
 powder
3 tablespoons water
boiling water

Serves 6
Slow cooking time : 4 hours

Rhubarb and Sultana Compote

METRIC/IMPERIAL
0.75 kg/1½ lb rhubarb
150 ml/¼ pint boiling water
100 g/4 oz granulated sugar
100 g/4 oz sultanas

Cut the rhubarb into 2.5-cm/1-inch lengths and place in the slow cooker with the water and sugar. Cover and cook on LOW for 4–5 hours. Stir in the sultanas and cook for a further 15 minutes.

Turn into a serving dish and leave to cool; serve with cream or ice cream.

AMERICAN
1½ lb fresh rhubarb
⅔ cup boiling water
½ cup sugar
1 cup seedless white raisins

Serves 4–6
Slow cooking time: 4¼–5¼ hours

Baked Apples

METRIC/IMPERIAL
4 medium cooking apples
50 g/2 oz soft brown sugar
50 g/2 oz raisins
¼ teaspoon ground cinnamon
25 g/1 oz butter
150 ml/¼ pint boiling water

Wash the apples and remove the cores. Make a shallow cut round the middle of each apple. Mix the sugar, raisins and cinnamon together. Put the apples in the slow cooker and pack the sugar and fruit mixture tightly into the centres. Top each apple with a knob of butter and pour round the boiling water. Cover and cook on LOW for 5 hours. Lift out with a slotted spoon to serve.

AMERICAN
4 medium baking apples
¼ cup soft brown sugar
½ cup raisins
¼ teaspoon ground cinnamon
2 tablespoons butter
⅔ cup boiling water

Serves 4
Slow cooking time: 5 hours

Winter Fruit Salad

METRIC/IMPERIAL
350 g/12 oz dried fruit salad
450 ml/¾ pint boiling water
312-g/11-oz can mandarin orange segments, drained
312-g/11-oz can lichees, drained
25 g/1 oz toasted almonds

Put the dried fruit salad into a bowl, cover with cold water and leave to soak overnight, then drain. Put the fruit salad into the slow cooker and cover with the boiling water. Cover and cook on LOW for 8–9 hours or until tender.

Turn out into a serving dish, stir in the mandarin orange segments and the lichees and chill thoroughly. Just before serving, scatter with the almonds and serve with plenty of cream.

AMERICAN
¾ lb mixed dried fruit (apple, apricots and prunes)
2 cups boiling water
11-oz can mandarin orange segments, drained
11-oz can lichee nuts, drained
¼ cup toasted almonds

Serves 6–8
Slow cooking time: 8–9 hours

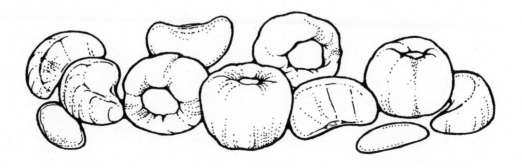

opposite *Winter Fruit Salad*
(page 97)

above *Spiced Apricots*
(page 100)

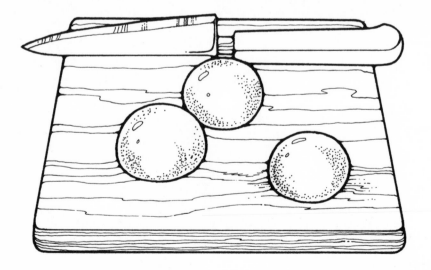

Spiced Apricots

METRIC/IMPERIAL
0.75 kg/1½ lb fresh apricots
75 g/3 oz castor sugar
300 ml/½ pint boiling water
¼ teaspoon ground cinnamon

Wash and peel apricots; place in the slow cooker with all the other ingredients. Cover and cook on LOW for 7–8 hours. Turn into a dish and leave to cool. Chill well and serve with lots of thick cream.

AMERICAN
1½ lb fresh apricots
6 tablespoons sugar
1¼ cups boiling water
¼ teaspoon ground cinnamon

Serves 6
Slow cooking time: 7–8 hours

Gooseberries with Elderflowers

METRIC/IMPERIAL
0.5 kg/1 lb gooseberries
150 ml/¼ pint boiling water
100 g/4 oz granulated sugar
2 sprigs elderflowers

The elderflowers give a lovely scent and flavour to the gooseberries.

Top and tail the gooseberries and wash well. Drain and put them in the slow cooker with the water and sugar. Tie the elderflowers in a small piece of muslin and add to the fruit. Cover and cook on LOW for 4–5 hours. Remove and discard the elderflowers, turn the gooseberries into a dish and leave to cool. Chill well and serve with cream.

AMERICAN
3 cups gooseberries
⅔ cup boiling water
½ cup sugar
2 sprigs elderflowers

Serves 4
Slow cooking time: 4–5 hours

Spotted Dick

METRIC/IMPERIAL
100 g/4 oz plain flour
1 teaspoon baking powder
100 g/4 oz fresh white
   breadcrumbs
100 g/4 oz shredded suet
50 g/2 oz castor sugar
100 g/4 oz mixed dried fruit
1 egg, beaten
150 ml/¼ pint milk
boiling water

Sift the flour and baking powder into a bowl, add the remaining dry ingredients and mix well. Stir in the egg and milk and mix thoroughly. Turn the mixture into a greased 900-ml/1½-pint (US 2-pint) pudding basin and cover with a piece of greased greaseproof paper and a lid of pleated foil.
   Stand the basin in the slow cooker on a jam jar lid and pour in sufficient boiling water to come halfway up the sides of the basin. Cover and cook on HIGH for 3½–4 hours. Run a knife round the sides of the basin to turn out. Serve with golden syrup.

AMERICAN
1 cup all-purpose flour
1 teaspoon baking powder
2 cups fresh white bread
   crumbs
scant cup chopped suet
¼ cup sugar
¾ cup mixed dried fruit
1 egg, beaten
⅔ cup milk
boiling water

Serves 6
Slow cooking time: 3½–4 hours

Christmas Pudding

METRIC/IMPERIAL
100 g/4 oz self-raising flour
½ teaspoon mixed spice
¼ teaspoon grated nutmeg
½ teaspoon salt
175 g/6 oz currants
175 g/6 oz sultanas
175 g/6 oz raisins
175 g/6 oz fresh white
    breadcrumbs
175 g/6 oz shredded suet
50 g/2 oz chopped mixed peel
50 g/2 oz almonds, blanched
    and chopped
1 small cooking apple, peeled,
    cored and grated
grated rind and juice of ½
    orange
225 g/8 oz soft brown sugar
3 eggs, beaten
5 tablespoons medium dry
    cider
 boiling water

This is an excellent way first to cook and then to heat your Christmas pudding – as the pudding takes care of itself, there is no need to remember to top up the water. On Christmas morning, put the pudding on and tuck it away in a corner of the kitchen, thus leaving yourself a spare ring on the cooker.

Grease a 1.5-litre/2½-pint (US 3-pint) pudding basin. Sift the flour, spices and salt together. Put the dried fruit into a bowl with the breadcrumbs, suet, peel, almonds, apple and orange rind and juice and stir in the spiced flour and brown sugar. Add the eggs and measured cider and stir thoroughly until well mixed. Turn into the prepared basin. Cover with greased greaseproof paper and a piece of pleated foil.

Stand the basin on a jam jar lid in the slow cooker and pour in sufficient boiling water to come halfway up the sides of the basin. Cover and cook on HIGH for 2 hours then turn to LOW for a further 8 hours. Lift the basin out of the pot, leaving the foil and greaseproof paper in place. Store until required.

To heat through: return to the pot, top up with boiling water, cover and cook on HIGH for 4 hours. The slow cooker can be turned to LOW and the pudding kept until required. Run a knife round the edge of the basin and turn out on to a warm serving dish. Serve with brandy butter and cream.

Serves 10
Slow cooking time: 10 hours (4 hours to reheat)

AMERICAN
1 cup all-purpose flour sifted
    with 1 teaspoon baking
    powder
½ teaspoon mixed spice
¼ teaspoon grated nutmeg
½ teaspoon salt
1 cup currants
1 cup seedless white raisins
1 cup raisins
3 cups fresh white bread
    crumbs
1¼ cups chopped suet
⅓ cup chopped candied peel
⅓ cup almonds, blanched and
    chopped
1 small baking apple, peeled,
    cored and grated
grated rind and juice of ½
    orange
1 cup soft brown sugar
3 eggs, beaten
6 tablespoons medium dry
    cider
boiling water

Peach Brûlée

METRIC/IMPERIAL
6 peaches
150 ml/¼ pint water
50 g/2 oz granulated sugar
strips of lemon rind
2 (150-ml/5-oz) cartons
    soured cream
100 g/4 oz brown sugar

This recipe makes a delicious dessert for guests at a summer dinner party when peaches are in season. The soured cream adds a refreshingly different touch to a simple but elegant dish.

Place the peaches in a bowl, cover with boiling water and leave to stand for 20 seconds. Transfer the peaches to a bowl of cold water, then peel, slice and lay the slices in the slow cooker. Put the measured water, white sugar and lemon rind in a small saucepan and bring to the boil, stirring to dissolve the sugar. Pour the syrup over the peaches, cover and cook on LOW for 2–3 hours (the time will vary according to the ripeness of the peaches).

Lift out the peach slices with a slotted spoon and place in a shallow ovenproof dish. Pour over the soured cream and sprinkle with brown sugar. Place under a hot grill and cook until the sugar bubbles and caramelises, then remove from the heat. Cool, then chill in the refrigerator.

Serves 4–6
Slow cooking time: 2–3 hours

AMERICAN
6 peaches
⅔ cup water
¼ cup sugar
strips of lemon rind
2 (5-oz) cartons dairy sour
    cream
½ cup brown sugar

Christmas Pudding (page 101)

Rhubarb and Orange Pudding

This is a great family favourite — the rhubarb and orange make a wonderful combination of flavours.

METRIC/IMPERIAL
175 g/6 oz self-raising flour
100 g/4 oz granulated sugar
50 g/2 oz shredded suet
grated rind and juice of 1 orange
175 g/6 oz rhubarb, cut in 1- cm/½-inch lengths
6 tablespoons milk and water mixed (approx.)
boiling water

AMERICAN
1½ cups all-purpose flour sifted with 1½ teaspoons baking powder
½ cup sugar
⅓ cup chopped suet
grated rind and juice of 1 orange
6 oz fresh rhubarb, cut in ½-inch lengths
½ cup milk and water mixed (approx.)
boiling water

Place the flour, sugar, suet and grated orange rind in a bowl and mix well. Stir in the orange juice, rhubarb and sufficient mixed milk and water to make a soft dropping consistency (the quantity of milk and water will vary with the size of the orange and the quantity of juice obtained from it).

Turn into a greased 900-ml/1½-pint (US 2-pint) basin and cover with a piece of greased greaseproof paper and a lid of pleated foil. Stand the basin on a jam jar lid in the slow cooker and add sufficient boiling water to come halfway up the sides of the basin. Cover and cook on HIGH for 3½–4 hours. Run a knife round the sides of the basin to turn the pudding out on to a serving dish. Serve with cream or custard.

Serves 6
Slow cooking time: 3½–4 hours

Sussex Pond Pudding

This is a simply gorgeous winter pudding. The butter and brown sugar melt, making a sauce to which the lemon adds bite.

METRIC/IMPERIAL
175 g/6 oz self-raising flour
75 g/3 oz shredded suet
150 ml/¼ pint milk (approx.)
75 g/3 oz butter
75 g/3 oz demerara sugar
1 large lemon
boiling water

AMERICAN
1½ cups all-purpose flour, sifted with 1½ teaspoons baking powder
½ cup chopped suet
⅔ cup milk (approx.)
⅓ cup butter
6 tablespoons light brown sugar
1 large lemon
boiling water

Mix the flour and suet together in a bowl and add sufficient milk to mix to a soft dough. Turn on to a floured surface and knead lightly. Cut off a quarter of the dough and put on one side. Roll out the remaining dough and use to line a buttered 900-ml/1½-pint (US 2-pint) pudding basin.

Cut the butter into small pieces and mix with the sugar. Prick the lemon all over with a fork and stand it upright in the centre of the basin. Put the butter and sugar mixture round the lemon.

Roll out the remaining piece of dough into a circle the size of the top of the basin and cover the pudding; damp the edges and seal firmly. Cover with a greased piece of pleated foil. Stand the basin in the slow cooker on a jam jar lid and pour in sufficient boiling water to come halfway up the sides of the pudding. Cover the pot and cook on HIGH for 4 hours.

Run a knife round the sides of the pudding and turn out on to a serving dish. When serving, make sure that each portion is garnished with a slice of the lemon from inside the pudding.

Serves 4
Slow cooking time: 4 hours

Apricot Lemon Pudding

METRIC/IMPERIAL
3 tablespoons apricot jam
1 tablespoon lemon juice
50 g/2 oz soft margarine
50 g/2 oz castor sugar
1 egg, beaten
50 g/2 oz self-raising flour
boiling water

Well butter a 600-ml/1 pint (US 1½-pint) pudding basin. Blend the apricot jam with the lemon juice and put in the basin. Cream the margarine and sugar until light and fluffy, then gradually beat in the egg, a little at a time. Fold in the flour and put the mixture in the basin; smooth the top.

Cover with a piece of greased greaseproof paper and a lid of pleated foil. Stand the basin on a jam jar lid in the slow cooker. Pour boiling water around the sides to come halfway up the basin. Cover and cook on HIGH for 3–4 hours. Run a knife round the sides of the basin to turn the pudding out on to a serving dish.

AMERICAN
4 tablespoons apricot jam
1 tablespoon lemon juice
¼ cup soft margarine
¼ cup sugar
1 egg, beaten
½ cup all-purpose flour sifted with ½ teaspoon baking powder
boiling water

Serves 2
Slow cooking time: 3–4 hours

Golden Sponge

METRIC/IMPERIAL
2 tablespoons golden syrup
100 g/4 oz soft margarine
100 g/4 oz castor sugar
2 eggs, beaten
100 g/4 oz self-raising flour
boiling water

Butter a 900-ml/1½-pint (US 2-pint) pudding basin and put the golden syrup in the base. Cream the margarine and sugar until light and fluffy, then gradually add the eggs a little at a time. Fold in the flour and turn the mixture into the basin; smooth the top and cover with a piece of greased greaseproof paper and a lid of pleated foil.

Stand the basin in the slow cooker on a jam jar lid and pour in sufficient boiling water to come halfway up the sides of the basin. Cover and cook on HIGH for 4 hours. Ease round the sides of the basin with a knife and turn out on to a serving dish.

AMERICAN
3 tablespoons corn syrup
½ cup soft margarine
½ cup sugar
2 eggs, beaten
1 cup all-purpose flour sifted with 1 teaspoon baking powder
boiling water

Serves 6
Slow cooking time: 4 hours

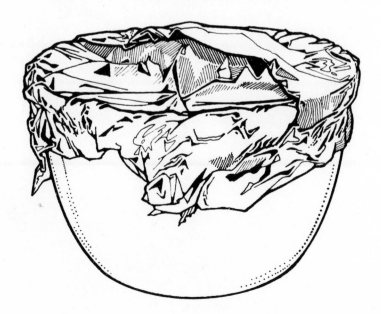

Rhubarb and Orange Pudding,
Apricot Lemon Pudding, Golden
Sponge in foil (pages 104–5)

Prunes with Almonds and Lemon

METRIC/IMPERIAL
350 g/12 oz prunes
150 ml/¼ pint boiling water
100 g/4 oz granulated sugar
strips of peel from ½ lemon
25 g/1 oz almonds

Leave the prunes to soak overnight, then drain well and put in the slow cooker with the boiling water, sugar and strips of lemon peel. Cover and cook on HIGH for 3 hours. Remove the lemon peel and turn into a serving dish, cool then chill well. When ready to serve, scatter over the almonds and serve with plenty of whipped cream.

AMERICAN
2 cups prunes
⅔ cup boiling water
½ cup sugar
strips of peel from ½ lemon
¼ cup almonds

Serves 4
Slow cooking time: 3 hours

Creamy Rice Pudding

METRIC/IMPERIAL
600 ml/1 pint milk
50 g/2 oz short-grain rice
50 g/2 oz castor sugar
15 g/½ oz butter
grated nutmeg

Put the milk, rice and sugar in a saucepan and bring to the boil, stirring. Pour into the slow cooker, dot with the butter and sprinkle with a little grated nutmeg. Cover and cook on LOW for 5–6 hours, stirring occasionally.

AMERICAN
2½ cups milk
¼ cup short-grain rice
¼ cup sugar
1 tablespoon butter
grated nutmeg

Serves 4
Slow cooking time: 5–6 hours

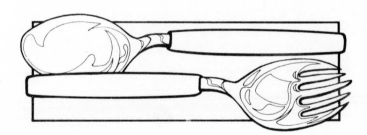

ONE POT SPECIALS

Other dishes, ranging from breakfasts to party meals, can also be made in the slow cooker, and this section includes recipes for such foods as scrambled egg, marmalade and porridge. Rice can be easily cooked in the pot for use with a meat dish. Bread rolls can be heated with flavourings such as garlic or cheese.

Another easy job for your slow cooker is saucemaking. Basic sauces and variations for any requirement, as well as bottled fruits, mulled wine, pâté, even cake and two exciting fondues complete the array of special dishes your versatile slow cooker can produce. Perhaps you'll come up with some other winners yourself.

Three-Fruit Marmalade, Lemon Curd (page 112)

Three-Fruit Marmalade

METRIC/IMPERIAL
1 kg/2 lb citrus fruit, including:
  1 grapefruit
  2 large lemons
  3 oranges
2 litres/3½ pints water
1.75 kg/4 lb granulated sugar

The joy of this recipe is that the kitchen is not full of steam while the fruit is cooking. Within the specified weight of citrus fruit, mix the fruit according to your taste.

AMERICAN
2 lb citrus fruit, including:
  1 grapefruit
  2 large lemons
  3 oranges
4½ pints water
8 cups sugar

Wash and dry the fruit and place in the slow cooker. Bring to the boil a scant 1.5 litres/2½ pints (US 6¼ cups) water. Pour over the fruit, cover and cook on LOW for 10–12 hours (overnight is ideal for this).

Lift all the fruit out into a colander, catching any juice in a bowl underneath, and return the juice to the pot. Cut the fruit in half, remove all the pips and white pith and put them in a small saucepan with the remaining measured water; simmer for 1 hour. Cut the peel into strips and put in a large pan with the liquid from the pot. Add the sugar. Strain the water from the pips and pith into the pan and bring to the boil, stirring until the sugar has dissolved; then boil rapidly.

Test for setting after 15 minutes: spoon a small amount of marmalade on to a cold saucer. When it is cool, the skin that forms on the surface will wrinkle when pushed with a finger if it has set. Pour into hot clean jars, cover and label.

Makes 2.75 kg/6 lb (US 8 cups) approx.
Slow cooking time: 10–12 hours

Lemon Curd

METRIC/IMPERIAL
100 g/4 oz butter
225 g/8 oz castor sugar
2 large lemons
2 large eggs or 4 egg yolks
150 ml/¼ pint boiling water

This is a lovely sharp lemon curd that will keep in a cool larder for up to 4 weeks, or in the refrigerator for 3 months.

AMERICAN
½ cup butter
1 cup sugar
2 large lemons
2 large eggs or 4 egg yolks
⅔ cup boiling water

Put the butter and sugar in a saucepan. Finely grate the rind and squeeze the juice from the lemons and stir into the pan. Place over a moderate heat and stir until the sugar has dissolved; allow to cool.

Beat the eggs or yolks lightly and stir into the pan. Pour into a 600-ml/1-pint (US 1½-pint) pudding basin and cover with foil. Stand the basin in the slow cooker on a jam jar lid and pour the boiling water in around it. Cover and cook on LOW for 4 hours, or until the mixture has thickened enough to coat the back of a wooden spoon. Pour into hot clean jars. Cover and label.

Makes 0.5 kg/1¼ lb (US 1⅔ cups) approx.
Slow cooking time: 4 hours

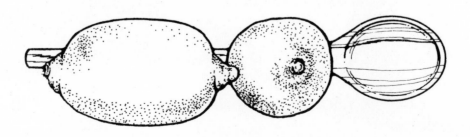

Scrambled Egg

METRIC/IMPERIAL
50 g/2 oz butter
8 eggs
6 tablespoons milk
salt and pepper

Very often eggs will stick when cooked in large quantities. The slow cooker cooks them easily and leaves them creamy and moist.

Well butter the base of the slow cooker and heat on HIGH for 10–15 minutes until the butter has melted. Beat the eggs with the milk and seasoning until well blended and pour into the pot. Cover and cook on HIGH for 30–40 minutes, stirring occasionally during the last 20 minutes of cooking time, until the eggs are thick and creamy. Serve on slices of hot buttered toast.

Serves 4
Slow cooking time: 40–55 minutes

AMERICAN
¼ cup butter
8 eggs
½ cup milk
salt and pepper

Porridge

METRIC/IMPERIAL
100 g/4 oz porridge oats
¼ teaspoon salt
600 ml/1 pint cold water

An ideal way to make deliciously creamy porridge – turn the slow cooker on just before going to bed, and in the morning breakfast is ready for the family to help themselves.

Place all the ingredients together in the slow cooker and stir well. Cover and cook on LOW for 8 hours or overnight. Stir well and serve with milk and plenty of brown sugar or golden syrup.

Serves 4
Slow cooking time: 8 hours

AMERICAN
⅔ cup oatmeal
¼ teaspoon salt
2½ cups cold water

Garlic Rolls

METRIC/IMPERIAL
50 g/2 oz butter
1 small clove garlic, crushed
salt
freshly ground black pepper
4 crisp white rolls

Use your slow cooker to heat rolls for breakfast: put the number required into the pot first thing in the morning, cover and cook on HIGH for 45 minutes to 1 hour. This method is ideal for warming rolls for dinner parties, barbecues and lunches.

Cream the butter until soft then beat in the garlic and seasoning. Make two cuts 2.5 cm/1 inch apart through each roll to within 1 cm/½ inch of the base and spread with the garlic butter. Wrap each roll loosely in foil, place in the slow cooker and cover. Cook on HIGH for 1 hour. Remove from the foil and serve with chops or pasta dishes.

Serves 4
Slow cooking time: 1 hour

AMERICAN
¼ cup butter
1 small clove garlic, crushed
salt
freshly ground black pepper
4 crisp white dinner rolls

Spiced Plums

METRIC/IMPERIAL
0.5 kg/1 lb plums
4 tablespoons malt vinegar
100 g/4 oz soft brown sugar
½ teaspoon mixed spice

These will keep, covered, in the refrigerator for at least 4 days and are lovely served with cold ham, tongue, poultry or veal.

AMERICAN
1 lb plums
⅓ cup malt vinegar
½ cup soft brown sugar
½ teaspoon mixed spice

Wash the plums, remove the stalks and place in the slow cooker with the vinegar, sugar and spice. Cover and cook on HIGH for 3 hours. Pour into a bowl (china or heatproof glass but not enamel), cover and leave to cool. Chill overnight in the refrigerator.

Makes 0.5 kg/1 lb
Slow cooking time: 3 hours

Apricots in Gin

METRIC/IMPERIAL
225 g/8 oz dried apricots
900 ml/1½ pints water
225 g/8 oz granulated sugar
4 tablespoons gin

These taste like apricots in brandy, as the gin takes on the flavour of the fruit. Serve with ice cream, whipped cream or in trifle.

AMERICAN
1½ cups dried apricots
3¾ cups water
1 cup sugar
⅓ cup gin

Put the apricots in a bowl, pour over two thirds of the water and leave to soak overnight; drain.

Put the remaining water in a pan with the sugar and bring slowly to the boil, stirring until the sugar has dissolved. Add the apricots, return to the boil and pour into the slow cooker. Cover and cook on HIGH for 2 hours. Unplug the pot and leave to stand for 2 hours.

Drain the apricots and divide between two 0.5-kg/1-lb screw top jars. Put the syrup into a small saucepan and boil rapidly until reduced by half; stir in the gin and pour over the apricots, making sure that they are completely covered. Screw the tops down firmly.

Makes 1 kg/2 lb
Slow cooking time: 2 hours

Prunes in Gin

METRIC/IMPERIAL
350 g/12 oz prunes
900 ml/1½ pints boiling water
225 g/8 oz granulated sugar
4 tablespoons gin

Put the prunes in a bowl with two thirds of the water and leave to soak for several hours or overnight. Drain well and put in the slow cooker with the remaining water and sugar. Cover and cook on HIGH for 3 hours. Unplug the pot and leave to cool for 2 hours.

AMERICAN
2 cups prunes
3¾ cups boiling water
1 cup sugar
⅓ cup gin

Drain the prunes and divide between two 0.5-kg/1-lb screw top jars. Place the prune syrup in a small pan and boil rapidly until reduced by half; stir in the gin and pour over the prunes. Seal well. Serve with whipped cream or ice cream.

Makes 1 kg/2 lb
Slow cooking time: 3 hours

opposite *Spiced Plums,*
Prunes in Gin

Baked Cottage Loaf

This makes a quick and economical supper for a hungry family.

Slice the loaf three times horizontally to give four pieces of bread. Layer with the fillings: on the base sprinkle the cheese then cover with the second piece of bread. Remove any rind and bone from the bacon, cut in thin strips and gently fry with the mushrooms until the fat runs out of the bacon; spread over the second piece of bread and cover with the next slice.

Finally fry the onions with the butter until soft, spread over the third piece of bread and cover with the final slice. Place in the slow cooker, cover and cook on HIGH for 2 hours. The cheese will melt and the other fillings will become hot. Serve cut in wedges with a green salad.

Serves 4
Slow cooking time: 2 hours

METRIC/IMPERIAL
1 cottage or cob loaf
Fillings:
50–75 g/2–3 oz Gouda cheese, grated
100 g/4 oz streaky bacon
50 g/2 oz button mushrooms, sliced
2 onions, sliced
25 g/1 oz butter

AMERICAN
1 cottage loaf or round bread
Fillings:
$\frac{1}{2}$–$\frac{3}{4}$ cup grated Gouda
6 slices bacon
$\frac{1}{2}$ cup sliced button mushrooms
2 onions, sliced
2 tablespoons butter

Bolognese Sauce

This recipe makes enough meat sauce for spaghetti for four people and for a lasagne for four, too. If you have a freezer, double up the recipe and freeze in four lots.

Heat the oil in a pan, add the bacon, beef and onions and fry, stirring frequently, until brown. Add the remaining ingredients and bring to the boil. Turn into the slow cooker, cover and cook on HIGH for 30 minutes, then turn to LOW for a further $2\frac{1}{2}$–3 hours. Taste to check the seasoning.

Serves 8
Slow cooking time: 3–3½ hours

METRIC/IMPERIAL
2 tablespoons cooking oil
100 g/4 oz streaky bacon, rinded and cut in strips
1 kg/2 lb minced beef
2 large onions, chopped
2 cloves garlic, crushed
1 teaspoon mixed dried herbs
2 teaspoons salt
1 teaspoon castor sugar
142-g/5-oz can tomato purée
450 ml/¾ pint water

AMERICAN
3 tablespoons cooking oil
6 slices bacon, rinded and cut in strips
2 lb ground beef
2 large onions, chopped
2 cloves garlic, crushed
1 teaspoon mixed dried herbs
2 teaspoons salt
1 teaspoon sugar
5-oz can tomato paste
2 cups water

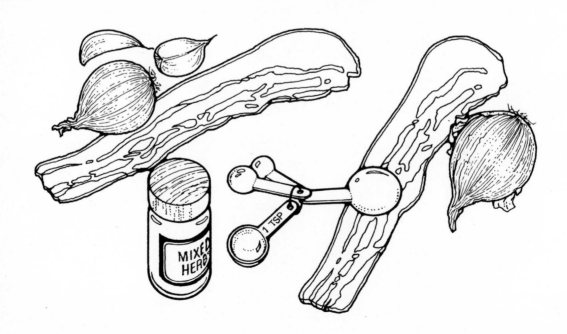

Espagnole Sauce

METRIC/IMPERIAL
75 g/3 oz dripping
75 g/3 oz streaky bacon, rinded and chopped
1 onion, chopped
2 sticks celery, chopped
100 g/4 oz mushrooms, sliced
75 g/3 oz plain flour
900 ml/1½ pints beef stock
1 tablespoon tomato purée
bay leaf
½ teaspoon dried thyme
large sprig parsley
¼ teaspoon pepper

AMERICAN
⅓ cup drippings
4 slices bacon, rinded and chopped
1 onion, chopped
2 stalks celery, chopped
1 cup sliced mushrooms
¾ cup all-purpose flour
4 cups beef stock
1 tablespoon tomato paste
bay leaf
½ teaspoon dried thyme
large sprig parsley
¼ teaspoon pepper

If you have a large slow cooker make up double the amount of sauce, divide it into six 300-ml/½-pint (US 1¼-cup) containers and freeze. Then use as required (see variations below).

Melt the dripping in a frying pan and fry the bacon for 2–3 minutes. Add the vegetables to the pan and cook gently for 5 minutes. Stir in the flour and cook slowly until browned, about 20 minutes. Stir in the stock and bring to the boil, stirring. Add the tomato purée, herbs and seasoning.

Turn into the slow cooker, cover and cook on HIGH for 30 minutes then turn to LOW and cook for a further 1½ hours. Strain through a sieve and divide into three 300-ml/½-pint (US 1¼-cup) containers. Or to use at once, add extra stock or wine as needed for the required consistency, reheat and serve.

Makes 900 ml/1½ pints (US 2 pints)
Slow cooking time: 2 hours

MADEIRA SAUCE

Add 3 tablespoons (US ¼ cup) Madeira wine to 300 ml/½ pint (US 1¼ cups) Espagnole sauce; heat and serve with ham.

SWEET AND SOUR SAUCE

Add 1 tablespoon soya sauce, 2 (US 3) tablespoons redcurrant jelly and 2 teaspoons vinegar to 300 ml/½ pint (US 1¼ cups) Espagnole sauce; heat and serve with bacon or pork.

LYONNAISE SAUCE

Add 100 g/4 oz (US ¼ lb) sliced fried onions and 4 tablespoons (US ⅓ cup) white wine to 300 ml/½ pint (US 1¼ cups) Espagnole sauce; heat and serve with meat or vegetables such as celery.

BIGARADE SAUCE

Add one finely chopped fried onion, 2 (US 3) tablespoons red wine, the rind and juice of one orange and 1 tablespoon redcurrant jelly to 300 ml/½ pint (US 1¼ cups) Espagnole sauce. Heat and serve with duck or game.

CHASSEUR SAUCE

Fry 100 g/4 oz (US 1 cup) sliced mushrooms in 1 tablespoon cooking oil with one finely chopped onion for 5 minutes. Stir in 4 tablespoons (US ⅓ cup) white wine and 2 teaspoons tomato purée, and add to 300 ml/½ pint (US 1¼ cups) Espagnole sauce; heat through. Just before serving stir in a knob of butter and a little chopped parsley. Serve with steaks.

opposite *Swiss Cheese Fondue* (page 120)

above *Baked Cottage Loaf* (page 116)

Swiss Cheese Fondue

METRIC/IMPERIAL
1 clove garlic, crushed
225 g/8 oz Emmenthal cheese, grated
225 g/8 oz Gruyère cheese, grated
300 ml/½ pint dry white wine
25 g/1 oz cornflour
salt and pepper
1 tablespoon Kirsch

Serve with lots of French bread cut in chunks to dip in the fondue.

Put the garlic and cheeses in the slow cooker. Heat all but 3 tablespoons (US ¼ cup) of the wine and pour into the pot; cover and cook on LOW for 1½ hours until the cheese has melted.

Turn the pot to HIGH. Blend the cornflour with the remaining wine and add a little of the hot mixture to it; stir into the pot. Stir occasionally until the sauce has thickened. Add seasoning and stir in the Kirsch. Serve immediately, or leave in the pot on LOW for up to 1 hour to keep warm.

AMERICAN
1 clove garlic, crushed
2 cups grated Emmenthal
2 cups grated Gruyère
1¼ cups dry white wine
¼ cup cornstarch
salt and pepper
1 tablespoon Kirsch

Serves 4–6
Slow cooking time: 2 hours

Chocolate Fondue

METRIC/IMPERIAL
large can evaporated milk
225 g/8 oz plain chocolate
225 g/8 oz icing sugar, sifted
25 g/1 oz cornflour
4 tablespoons rum or brandy

This fondue is very rich and will serve 12–15 people. It also makes a delicious sauce to serve with pears and ice cream.

Pour the evaporated milk into the slow cooker and cook on LOW for 30 minutes. Break the chocolate into pieces, add to the milk, cover and cook on LOW for a further 1½ hours.

Turn the pot to HIGH. Stir the chocolate and milk mixture with a small whisk until well blended, then work in the icing sugar. Blend the cornflour with the rum or brandy and a little of the chocolate. Whisk into the mixture in the pot. Cover and cook on HIGH for 30–45 minutes until the chocolate has thickened, stirring occasionally.

Serve in the pot with plenty of sponge finger biscuits or marshmallows on cocktail sticks to dip into the fondue.

AMERICAN
large can evaporated milk
1⅓ cups semi-sweet chocolate pieces
2 cups sifted confectioners' sugar
¼ cup cornstarch
⅓ cup rum or brandy

Serves 12–15
Slow cooking time: 2½–2¾ hours

One Pot Rice

METRIC/IMPERIAL
225 g/8 oz long-grain rice
750 ml/1¼ pints boiling water
1 teaspoon salt

A very easy way to cook rice – let the slow cooker do the work for you.

Put the rice in the slow cooker, pour over the boiling water and add the salt; stir lightly with a fork. Cover and cook on HIGH for 1 hour, then turn the pot down to LOW and cook for a further 30–40 minutes, until all the water has been absorbed. Stir occasionally with a fork.

The rice will keep satisfactorily for a further 30 minutes on LOW, but after a longer time it tends to stick to the sides of the pot.

Serves 4
Slow cooking time: 1½–1¾ hours

AMERICAN
1 cup long-grain rice
1½ pints boiling water
1 teaspoon salt

Mulled Wine

METRIC/IMPERIAL
2 lemons
1 litre/1¾ pints red wine
600 ml/1 pint water
8 cloves
¼ teaspoon ground cinnamon
50–100 g/2–4 oz castor sugar
2 tablespoons cheap brandy

The slow cooker keeps mulled wine gently hot for serving. Don't forget to add the brandy (or sherry) to make it potent.

Peel the zest very thinly from the lemons, cut a few slices of lemon for garnish, then squeeze the remainder to extract the juice. Put the lemon zest, juice, wine and water with the cloves and cinnamon into the slow cooker.

Cover and cook on HIGH for 30 minutes, then turn to LOW for 1½ hours. Lift out the lemon zest and cloves and add sugar to taste. Serve hot with the slices of lemon floating on top. Add the brandy just before serving.

AMERICAN
2 lemons
2 pints red wine
2½ cups water
8 cloves
¼ teaspoon ground cinnamon
¼–½ cup sugar
3 tablespoons cheap brandy

Serves 8
Slow cooking time: 2 hours

Peter's Pâté

METRIC/IMPERIAL
275 g/10 oz pig's liver
1 small onion
225 g/8 oz pork sausagemeat
½ teaspoon salt
freshly ground black pepper
1½ tablespoons chopped fresh
　mixed herbs
1 clove garlic, crushed
1 egg, beaten
streaky bacon rashers
boiling water

Mince the liver and onion finely and mix with the sausagemeat, seasoning, herbs and garlic. Bind with the beaten egg.

Line a 0.5-kg/1-lb loaf tin, terrine or 15-cm/6-inch cake tin (to fit your slow cooker) with rashers of streaky bacon. Press in the mixture and smooth the top, then cover with a lid of foil.

Put the container in the slow cooker and pour in enough boiling water to come halfway up the sides of the tin. Cover the pot and cook on LOW for 5 hours. Remove the pâté from the slow cooker and leave to cool in the tin. Put a weight on top and chill for several hours.

Turn out and serve sliced, with hot toast or French bread.

AMERICAN
10 oz pork liver
1 small onion
1 cup pork sausagemeat
½ teaspoon salt
freshly ground black pepper
2 tablespoons chopped fresh
　mixed herbs
1 clove garlic, crushed
1 egg, beaten
bacon slices
boiling water

Serves 8–10
Slow cooking time: 5 hours

Aubergine Caviar

METRIC/IMPERIAL
2–3 aubergines
1 clove garlic, crushed
1 small onion, very finely
　chopped
1 small green pepper, seeded
　and very finely chopped
freshly ground black pepper
salt
lemon juice

This unusual way of using aubergines when they are in season adds interest to a buffet or drinks party.

Place the whole aubergines in the slow cooker, cover and cook on HIGH for 2½–3 hours until soft (the time will vary with the size of the aubergines). Cool then split the aubergines and scrape out the insides with a stainless steel or silver spoon (this helps prevent discoloration).

Chop the aubergines and turn into a bowl. Add the remaining ingredients with lemon juice to taste and sharpen the flavour. Turn into a smaller bowl, chill well and serve with hot toast and butter.

AMERICAN
2–3 eggplant
1 clove garlic, crushed
1 small onion, very finely
　chopped
1 small green pepper, seeded
　and very finely chopped
freshly ground black pepper
salt
lemon juice

Serves 4
Slow cooking time: 2½–3 hours

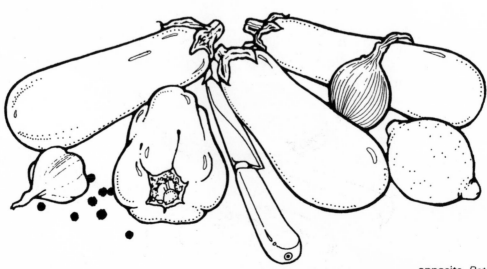

opposite *Peter's Pâté*

Swiss Almond Carrot Cake

METRIC/IMPERIAL

METRIC/IMPERIAL
5 eggs, separated
275 g/10 oz castor sugar
grated rind of ½ lemon
275 g/10 oz ground almonds
250 g/9 oz carrots, peeled and
    grated
50 g/2 oz plain flour
1 teaspoon baking powder
boiling water
Topping:
apricot jam
175 g/6 oz icing sugar
2 tablespoons lemon juice

Well grease a 20-cm/8-inch round cake tin and line with greased greaseproof paper. Beat together the egg yolks and sugar until pale and creamy, then add the lemon rind, ground almonds, grated carrots and flour sifted with the baking powder. Whisk the egg whites until stiff and fold into the mixture, turn into the cake tin and smooth the top. Cover with a piece of greased foil and place on a jam jar lid in the slow cooker. Pour in sufficient boiling water to come halfway up the sides of the tin. Cover and cook on HIGH for 4 hours. Turn out and leave to cool on a wire rack.

When cold, brush the cake with a little warmed apricot jam. Blend the icing sugar with the lemon juice and use it to coat the top of the cake. Leave to set then store in an airtight tin for at least one day before eating.

Slow cooking time: 4 hours

AMERICAN
5 eggs, separated
1¼ cups sugar
grated rind of ½ lemon
2½ cups ground almonds
generous ½ lb carrots, peeled
    and grated
½ cup all-purpose flour
1 teaspoon baking powder
boiling water
Topping:
apricot jam
1⅓ cups confectioners' sugar
3 tablespoons lemon juice

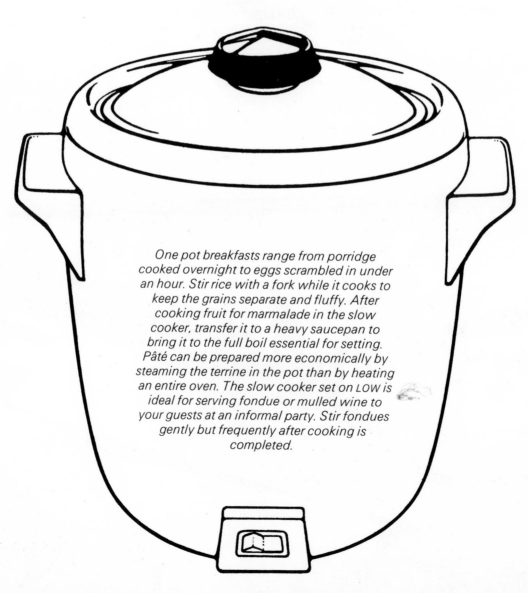

One pot breakfasts range from porridge cooked overnight to eggs scrambled in under an hour. Stir rice with a fork while it cooks to keep the grains separate and fluffy. After cooking fruit for marmalade in the slow cooker, transfer it to a heavy saucepan to bring it to the full boil essential for setting. Pâté can be prepared more economically by steaming the terrine in the pot than by heating an entire oven. The slow cooker set on LOW is ideal for serving fondue or mulled wine to your guests at an informal party. Stir fondues gently but frequently after cooking is completed.

Index

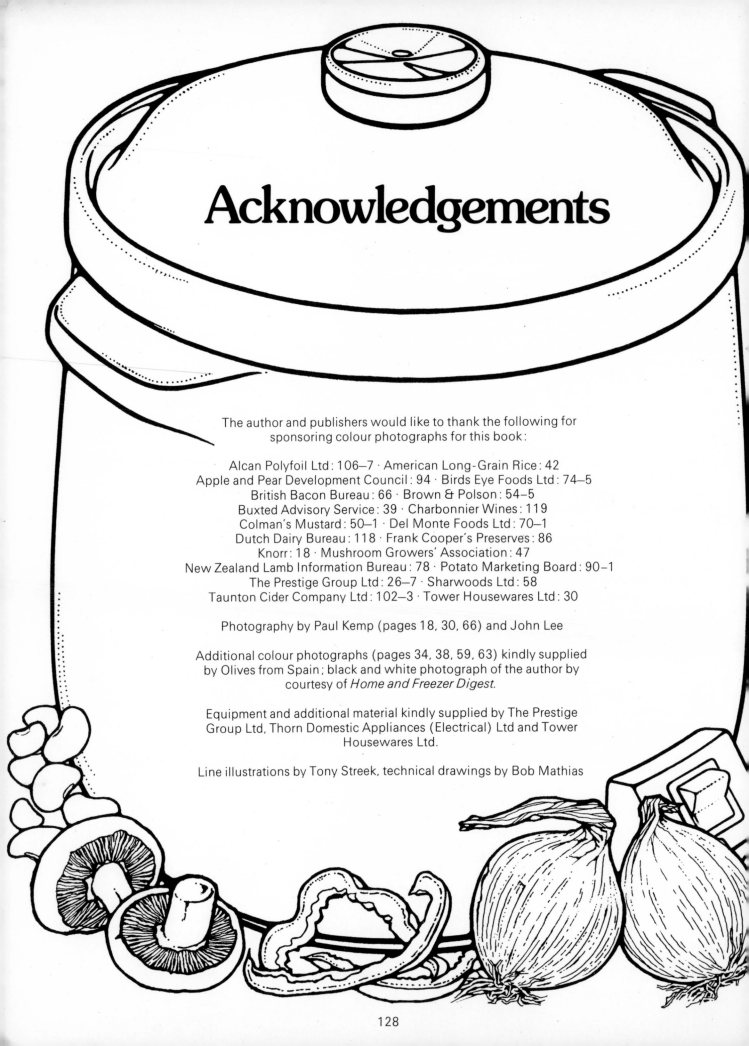

Acknowledgements

The author and publishers would like to thank the following for sponsoring colour photographs for this book:

Alcan Polyfoil Ltd: 106–7 · American Long-Grain Rice: 42
Apple and Pear Development Council: 94 · Birds Eye Foods Ltd: 74–5
British Bacon Bureau: 66 · Brown & Polson: 54–5
Buxted Advisory Service: 39 · Charbonnier Wines: 119
Colman's Mustard: 50–1 · Del Monte Foods Ltd: 70–1
Dutch Dairy Bureau: 118 · Frank Cooper's Preserves: 86
Knorr: 18 · Mushroom Growers' Association: 47
New Zealand Lamb Information Bureau: 78 · Potato Marketing Board: 90–1
The Prestige Group Ltd: 26–7 · Sharwoods Ltd: 58
Taunton Cider Company Ltd: 102–3 · Tower Housewares Ltd: 30

Photography by Paul Kemp (pages 18, 30, 66) and John Lee

Additional colour photographs (pages 34, 38, 59, 63) kindly supplied
by Olives from Spain; black and white photograph of the author by
courtesy of Home and Freezer Digest.

Equipment and additional material kindly supplied by The Prestige
Group Ltd, Thorn Domestic Appliances (Electrical) Ltd and Tower
Housewares Ltd.

Line illustrations by Tony Streek, technical drawings by Bob Mathias